D0372431

**NEWBORN**

# NEWBORN
## JACK HAYFORD

Tyndale House Publishers, Inc.
Wheaton, Illinois

"The Gospel of John" is taken from *The Living Bible,* copyright 1971 by Tyndale House Publishers, Wheaton, Illinois, and reprinted by permission.

All Bible quotations are taken from *The Living Bible,* copyright 1971 by Tyndale House Publishers, Wheaton, Illinois, unless indicated as being from *The Holy Bible,* New King James Version (NKJV), copyright 1979, 1980, 1982 by Thomas Nelson, Inc., Nashville, Tennessee.

First printing, Tyndale House edition, February 1987

Library of Congress Catalog Card Number 86-51349
ISBN 0-8423-4677-5
Copyright 1984 by Jack Hayford
All rights reserved
Printed in the United States of America

# CONTENTS

# CHAPTER ONE
# THE FAMILY'S WELCOME

Welcome, friend!

You're the reason this little book was written, to welcome you into the family of God. So, welcome!

Because you have accepted Jesus Christ as your Savior, a new relationship with God and with his family is now open to you. And as a newborn family member, I want to tell you about us—that is you and me—all of us who have become members of the family.

When we refer to people who've accepted Christ as their Lord as family, we aren't being either sentimental or exclusive. In this case, "family" is more than just a figure of speech—it's an expression taken from the Bible. It is how the

Word of God describes those of us who have been "born again" into God's family:

> Now you are no longer strangers to God and foreigners to heaven, but you are members of God's very own family, citizens of God's country, and you belong in God's household with every other Christian. (Ephesians 2:19)

And so I'm welcoming you to new relationships.

Through this booklet, I hope to help acquaint you with the dimensions, values, meanings, and possibilities that are open to you as a "newborn" member of God's family. So, welcome to the family of God, where you will discover both a new quantity of life—eternal life—and new qualities of life.

## WHAT JESUS BRINGS TO YOUR LIFE

Regardless of our individual stories, we all share in the common experience of sin. When we sin, we miss a mark or fall short of a goal or standard. And sin shows up in all of us, at our best and at our worst.

At best, our lives are finite and limited, cluttered with failure and the underlying feeling that life is not all that it should be. Few people seem to taste of what God really intended us to know in terms of life's purpose and fulfillment. At worst, we spend too much time in pursuit of blurred or deceptive goals, resulting in disappointment, sin, and personal bondage. In either case, sin and its consequences afflict every one of us.

But God's Son, Jesus Christ, stepped into this human dilemma telling us that he came to open up life in all of its abundance and meaning: "My purpose is to give life in all its fullness" (John 10:10). This abundant, full life Christ offers us has a double dimension.

First, it addresses the endless future. It brings the hope of an eternal, unlimited experience in the fullness of God's joy. The Bible describes heaven as a "prepared place," promising us that God will ultimately gather us, his family, there. On the basis of Christ's promise in John 14:2, 3, we know we will be in heaven forever with our Lord (see also 1 Thessalonians 4:16, 17).

Second, it addresses the present. We are given the promise of abundant life here and now. Some people mistakenly think that life with Christ will only take place in heaven and that this present life is just something to be endured. Their false assumptions cause them to offer the philosophical advice to "Cheer up! Slog on through life as best you can. Someday, in heaven, it'll all be better." I want you to know, Newborn, that while our "someday" in heaven will be great, we are also promised a great life right now! If we follow Christ's instructions to live daily with him, then we will discover the triumph and joy there is in being a part of God's family, today.

## WHAT IT MEANS TO BE NEWBORN

Being newborn, or "born again," means that your inner spirit has been brought into a new relationship with God through the sacrifice of his Son, Jesus Christ.

When God first designed you, he intended you to be in close fellowship and friendship with him. But when you fell into disobedience and sin, as all of us have done, the contact with God was broken.

You should not condemn yourself for your failure, but you do need to be honest and acknowledge the truth of Romans 3:12, 17, 23: "Everyone has turned away; all have gone wrong. No one anywhere has kept on doing what is right; not one . . . and they have never known what it is to feel secure or enjoy God's blessing. . . . Yes, all have sinned; all fall short of God's glorious ideal."

Simply stated, God's Word is saying that none of us lives up to what God created us to be. When we understand and acknowledge that fact, we are ready to respond to the reason Jesus came. Christ's redemptive life, death, and resurrection were specifically provided so that we could return to the Father's original plans for us—plans that had us in vital, restoring, creative touch with him.

Now that you've decided to accept Jesus Christ as your Savior, your relationship with God is established. The moment you made that decision and believed in and committed your life to

Christ, God accomplished several things for you:

1. *Redemption: You are forgiven of sin.* "So overflowing is his kindness toward us that he took away all our sins through the blood of his Son, by whom we are saved" (Ephesians 1:7).

2. *Cleansing: You are washed from your sin.* "He saved us—not because we were good enough to be saved, but because of his kindness and pity—by washing away our sins and giving us the new joy of the indwelling Holy Spirit" (Titus 3:5).

3. *Regeneration: You are born anew.* "Jesus replied, 'What I am telling you so earnestly is this: Unless one is born of water and the Spirit, he cannot enter the Kingdom of God' " (John 3:5).

4. *Justification: You have peace with God.* "So now, since we have been made right in God's sight by faith in his promises, we can have real peace with him because of what Jesus Christ our Lord has done for us" (Romans 5:1).

5. *Adoption: You become one of God's children.* "And so we should not be like cringing, fearful slaves, but we should behave like God's very own children, adopted into the bosom of his family, and calling to him, 'Father, Father' " (Romans 8:15).

6. *Acceptance: You are received by the Father.* "His unchanging plan has always been to adopt us into his own family by sending Jesus Christ to die for us. And he did this because he wanted to! Now all praise to God for his wonderful kindness

to us and his favor that he has poured out upon us, because we belong to his dearly loved Son" (Ephesians 1:5, 6).

7. *Eternal Life: You have an endless hope.* "I say emphatically that anyone who listens to my message and believes in God who sent me has eternal life, and will never be damned for his sins, but has already passed out of death into life" (John 5:24).

All these things are yours now, for you have received Jesus Christ, acknowledging him as God's Son who died on the cross for our sins and who has risen from the dead. These are the beginnings of the blessings included in the gift of salvation. They comprise what it basically means when we use the expression "I'm saved!"

So now that you are beginning your new life through Christ, you will find God's Holy Spirit continually helping you increase your understanding of your new Father and family. The Spirit will widen your viewpoint on the greatness of our heavenly Father's love and grace.

It was through the Holy Spirit that God first spoke to your heart and called you to life with him. When you responded, you said in essence, "I want the Lord Jesus Christ in my life. I want to know God's love and forgiveness." This decision was the first step that you and millions of others have taken, a step of faith into a family of brothers and sisters who have come to know the heavenly Father in a personal, powerful way.

And, since you are being introduced to a new

family, I thought it might be helpful for you to learn some of the household principles, some of the ways we in the family of God live "around the house." You can use this booklet as a basic guide into a whole new dimension of life where the goals are growth in Christ and further discovery of the kind of life we share in the family of God. And, you can use it as a pointer to God's Word, for it is his Word that opens new dimensions of meaning and heights of purpose in life, all of which you were given the right to explore when you received Jesus as your Savior and Lord.

# CHAPTER TWO
# THE FAMILY'S FATHER

The first basic element for living in God's family is to grow in your acquaintance with our heavenly Father. You accomplish this through conversation with him. In the Bible, Paul the apostle described this kind of friendship: "When I think of the wisdom and scope of his [God's] plan I fall down on my knees and pray to the Father of all the great family of God" (Ephesians 3:14, 15).

Paul not only mentions the family's Father, but shows the way to get to know him well. This way is something that is both a great privilege and a fundamental need for growth in Christ: prayer. Even as our physical bodies require breathing, our spirits require prayer.

Jesus has instructed us to freely approach our Father God, knowing we are welcome when we come "in Jesus' name." In John 16:24 he said, "Ask, using my name, and you will receive, and your cup of joy will overflow."

Suppose you were to stop at my parents' home and say, "Mr. and Mrs. Hayford, your son, Jack, told me that if I was ever in this area and needed food or a place to stay, that you would help me." If you came to them like this, I can assure you that they would welcome you. They might place a phone call and check to see if I really know you, but all I would need to say is, "Yes, I know this person. He's coming in my name, so please receive him." That would settle it. My parents love me, and the fact that you came "in my name" would give you immediate entrance into their home and certain care at their hands.

The Bible says we have been given the privilege of coming to the heavenly Father in the name of his Son, Jesus Christ. There is nothing in and of ourselves that warrants our acceptance or that grants us audience with God. When we pray we are not approaching some Wizard of Oz- or Santa Claus-type deity. We are approaching the Creator of the universe, who is righteous, holy, and almighty. Too often we have a warped image of God as either a fairy-tale figure, or as a distant, scowling authority figure. But Jesus came to help us see God as he really is. He takes both God's love and his authority and balances all this out for us. He introduces us to God's loving heart (see 1 John 1:18) and brings us into our Father's welcoming presence (see John 16:26, 27).

Because of our forgiveness through Christ (see Revelation 1:5), and because we claim no self-righteousness, we can come to the Father completely pure and acceptable. He welcomes us in Jesus' name, lovingly encouraging our fellowship with himself and promising to give us whatever we need when we ask in prayer (see Romans 8:31, 32).

But prayer is far more than merely asking God for things. Through prayer we can consult God, we can seek his direction in our everyday living. If you're a student, ask him to help you in school matters. If you're an employee or businessman, ask his blessing in your daily work and decision-making. If you're a parent, ask him to give you wisdom in raising your children, managing your household, and meeting the practical and financial needs of your family. When trouble, crisis, or any other need arises—whatever it is that concerns you—bring it to God in prayer.

> Ask, and you will be given what you ask for. Seek, and you will find. Knock, and the door will opened. For everyone who asks, receives. Anyone who seeks, finds. If only you will knock, the door will open. If a child asks his father for a loaf of bread, will he be given a stone instead? If he asks for fish, will he be given a poisonous snake? Of course not! And if you hardhearted, sinful men know how to give good gifts to your children, won't your Father in heaven even more certainly give

good gifts to those who ask him for them? (Matthew 7:7-11)

And it is he [God] who will supply all your needs from his riches in glory, because of what Christ Jesus has done for us. (Philippians 4:19)

## GROWING IN PARTNERSHIP

God invites us, through the privilege of prayer, to grow in partnership with him. You see, God could just stand in heaven and sprinkle things out of the sky like a man in a helicopter tossing bubble gum to kids on the street. But he doesn't deal with us in this way. Instead, he invites us to enter into an understanding, growing partnership. Through such Scripture passages as Ephesians 1 and Romans 8, we can see that God wants us to grow as family members. As you come to him in prayer, you will learn of his ways and his interest in you, as well as his purpose in creating you.

And when you pray, don't worry about using "spiritual" speech or fancy words. Just pray with all your heart, speaking out honestly and sharing what you are thinking and feeling. As you come before God in prayer, you will find that you have ready entrance and open access to him. So come obediently and with praise, for we are told to "enter his gates with thanksgiving and his courts with praise; give thanks to him and praise his name, for the Lord is good . . ." (Psalm 100:4, 5).

Why not pause right now and take time to speak your heart to your new family's Father. He is not hesitant to answer or give to us, his children, but he does expect us to come to him in prayer and loving worship.

# CHAPTER THREE
# THE FAMILY'S DIET

> The Scriptures tell us that bread won't feed men's souls: obedience to every word of God is what we need. (Matthew 4:4)

When Jesus said this he clearly intended us to understand that, as members of God's family, we can't survive without a daily diet of God's Word. In the Bible, God has given us far more than just a collection of stories or historical facts. He has given us his Word as spiritual food to nourish us, help us grow, and teach us his ways and will for our lives.

I want to encourage you to know his Word. You can start by turning now to the Gospel of John (included at the end of this book). As you open to chapter one, look at the wonder of the truths contained there. John begins by telling us that before the world was created, the Word—used here as a title for Christ—already existed with God. The following verses go on to explain the divine nature and glory of Jesus, his role in the creation of the universe, and the beauty of his person.

Then in verse 12, the Word speaks directly to us: "But to all who received him, he gave the right to become children of God. . . ." This statement declares that we are brought into God's family by our acceptance of Christ. Pause with me and prayerfully thank him for that! (Really, do! Just whisper a "thank you" to God for his love and forgiveness.)

Now, as one of God's children, you need to grow. And this spiritual growth comes in the same way as your physical growth: through eating. The Bible is your spiritual diet.

> As newborn babes, desire the pure milk
> of the Word, that you may grow thereby.
> (1 Peter 2:2, NKJV)

## BEGINNING IN THE BIBLE

One way to get into God's Word is to read through the Gospel of John during the next seven days. There are twenty-one chapters, so three chapters a day will do it. This may sound like a lot, but you will find that the thoughtful reading of three chapters takes less than fifteen minutes a day. You can accomplish that easily, and at the same time make an excellent beginning of a lifetime habit.

When you've finished the Gospel of John, read the following book—The Acts of the Apostles (the fifth book in the New Testament). The Gospel of John describes Jesus' life given to mankind; the Book of Acts describes Jesus' life living through mankind. As you read this second book, you will not only discover how to live as a follower of Christ, but you will enjoy reading how his first followers discovered God's glory and power filling their hearts and homes. The Word of God was their nourishment and the love and power of the Holy Spirit filled their lives daily (see Acts 2:42, 46, 47).

If you continue reading three chapters a day, it will take you about nine days to go through the Book of Acts. When you've finished with that book, turn to the beginning of the New Testament and read straight through it. You'll love the action and the truth you discover! But most of all you'll discover a hidden benefit: a progressive release through God's Word.

Jesus said, "And you will know the truth, and the truth will set you free" (John 8:32). Life in Christ is progressive and transforming. When you know his Word you will know how to live on his terms, in his truth, and in his triumph. Keep moving forward and don't be discouraged if you miss a day. Just start again and press on.

One thing you should know is that our common enemy, Satan, will try to obstruct your progress (see 1 Peter 5:8). But God, through his Word, will lead you into victory over the enemy (see Ephesians 6:16, 17; Romans 10:17).

After you've read the New Testament, begin reading the Old Testament. You can intersperse rereading the New Testament books with the Old Testament. This will help you expand your understanding of God's heart as well as his ways. The further you go into God's Word the more you will grow, and the more you will find the joy of knowing the Scriptures and receiving good spiritual nutrition.

# CHAPTER FOUR
# THE FAMILY'S FELLOWSHIP

Healthy families gather together regularly. As members of God's family, we each need the love, strength, and encouragement of solid, reinforcing fellowship. None of us can dare to give in to the temptation to be aloof or independent, or to withdraw.

Start with a lesson from Jesus' habit. He gathered regularly with those who wanted to know God's Word and to learn how to walk in his way (see Luke 4:16). We should follow his example. This doesn't mean that regular church attendance—simply putting in an appearance—has any special merit in itself. The real power of going to church is in what happens where living fellowship is experienced among people who are committed to Christ.

Being with people who worship and love the

Lord is contagious in a positive sense. If you are in a room with people who have measles, you're probably going to catch measles! Likewise, if you regularly gather with people who are growing, loving, and serving the Lord, you're going to "catch" that kind of life.

Unfortunately, many people today consider church synonymous with ritualism. Religious formality—"churchianity" some call it—has discouraged many from even bothering with church anymore. But the difference between a ritualistic gathering and a healthy, spiritual togetherness is readily discerned. I urge you toward consistent church attendance, not as a religious practice but as obedience to a biblical command: "Let us not neglect our church meetings, as some people do, but encourage and warn each other, especially now that the day of [Jesus'] coming back again is drawing near" (Hebrews 10:25).

Note that the Bible urges our regular fellowship because "the day" is coming. That day is explained in the Bible as being the ultimate day when each of us will stand before the Lord Jesus. It will be a day of rejoicing, for we shall stand without guilt before God. But we are also told that on that final day, each of us, as God's servants, will be required to give him an accounting of our lives.

We should not fear this, for our sins have already been forgiven and our acceptance before God is forever established through Christ. The question of judgment against us as sinners has been settled. But we will be called to account for our servanthood as followers of Christ—and that should prompt our wise sensitivity, faithful service, and obedient living.

So let us live as Christ's followers and servants, spending time in strengthening fellowship with one another. This way, we will be prepared to stand in his presence at his return and give a confident account of how we used the life he has given us.

> May the Lord make your love to grow and overflow to each other and to everyone else, just as our love does toward you. This will result in your hearts being made strong, sinless and holy by God our Father, so that you may stand before him guiltless on that day when our Lord Jesus Christ returns with all those who belong to him. (1 Thessalonians 3:12, 13)

## FINDING A PLACE OF FELLOWSHIP

The newborn believer needs the family's care, and the family rejoices in the increased learning that each new relationship brings. Simply stated, you and I need the church, and the church needs us. Even though I've never met you, I do know one thing: I can tell you from the depths of my heart that I love you.

You might wonder, "Jack, how can that be? You don't even know me." But that doesn't make any difference. You see, we've been born into the same family, and I can say I love you because the Holy Spirit of God who has made the life of Christ real in me affirms that you share his life too. By that inner awareness he creates a sense of family unity. And there are others near you who will show you this same love and care. There's a pastor and a group of believers who love Jesus and who the Lord wants to use to help you. So let them do that, because we do care about your persevering and going on, growing in the family.

As you seek a place of fellowship, allow the Holy Spirit to help you recognize the right church for your needs. I just encourage you to be sure you choose a place where they worship the living God; where they exalt the name of Jesus, honoring him as Savior and Lord; where the Word of God is preached and made the guidebook for all of your life; and where integrity of heart and purity of relationships are demonstrated and fostered in the love of God's Spirit.

I assure you, my newborn friend, in such a setting you can't help but grow. You will enjoy the reality of being in God's family and rejoice that when this life concludes we will be gathered together with God—forever.

# CHAPTER FIVE
# THE FAMILY'S CELEBRATION

Jesus said that heaven rejoices every time someone accepts him as their Savior. Our repentance causes great joy and celebration around God's throne. And Jesus calls us to a celebration here on earth as well—a celebration at which the whole family gathers and rejoices with you in your obedience to Christ's command: Your water baptism.

It may sound strange to call water baptism a "celebration," but that's exactly what it is. It isn't just a church ritual, and it was never intended just to be a part of joining a church or a lovely ceremony. Jesus calls us to water baptism immediately after we've been born again as a statement that we are now his followers (see Mark 16:16; Acts 8:35-38). (And even if you've had a ritual baptism earlier in your life, it isn't disrespectful for you to come as a newborn babe in Christ to be baptized again.)

Jesus commanded us to participate in water baptism because it is *spiritually dynamic.* It is an exercise in obedience indicating that you have turned from your past to Jesus. And it can cause a release in your soul whereby you sever bonds to your past and make room for the Holy Spirit's unrestricted presence in your life. When you are immersed in the waters of baptism, you are announcing, "My former life of self-will and sin is being buried in these waters as though they are buried in a tomb." And similarly, through the power of Jesus' resurrection, when you come up out of the water you declare a victory of renewal: you choose from that moment to live with Christ, free from the failure and bondage of your past (see Romans 6:4).

First you need to seek a place near you to be baptized, possibly at a church that you will begin to attend regularly. Respond to Jesus' command to be baptized, and share in that joyful celebration with others in the family who will love you and care about your beginning steps of obedience to Christ.

To receive the full spiritual impact and impression of Christ's purpose at your baptism in water, you need to understand what is happening. You need to come with an open heart and an awareness of God's provision for you. When you obey him and come before him in childlike trust, you open the door so that everything God intended to happen at your baptism can indeed happen!

Your baptism can be all that God intended it to be!

Your responsibility is obedience; God's responsibility is to take care of the results. At your baptism, he will be faithful to do his work. As faithful to you as he has been to all who have obediently responded to his command to be baptized.

## UNDERSTANDING WATER BAPTISM

Let's study further what water baptism is about. The rich yet simple power of this experience can be discovered in the Word of God. Through studying what God says about baptism we can avoid the confusion of the empty traditions that dilute or merely ceremonialize this experience.

As an ordinance or a command the Lord has given to those who follow him, you must take water baptism seriously. As a rite or practice observed in a sacred ceremony, you should approach water baptism reverently.

But your sobriety doesn't have to be somber, nor does your reverence need to be coldly ritualistic. For this moment is designed by God to be one of victory, rejoicing, and triumph! Expect to be happy, for heaven is rejoicing over your obedience. As you approach this holy moment, don't worry about being unduly "religious," as though God is watching to see how piously you can act. Simply come to the waters of baptism ready, joyful, and willing.

## BAPTISM AND SALVATION

At this point, we need to make a very clear distinction between baptism and salvation.

Baptism is an affirmation; a positive declaration or assertion. It is a statement made by both word and deed, declaring what you believe and to whom you have committed your life and eternal destiny. It is not the moment when your sins are forgiven, but rather the occasion you declare your lifelong commitment to God. This is why water baptism is intended to follow a decision to receive God's gift of salvation through the Lord Jesus.

In water baptism you affirm that you are saved by grace, and that what you are saved from is eternal death: "But God showed his great love for us by sending Christ to die for us while we were still sinners. And since by his blood he did all this for us as sinners, how much more will he do for us now that he has declared us not guilty? Now he will save us from all of God's wrath to come. And since, when we were his enemies, we were brought back to God by the death of his Son, what blessings he must have for us now that we are his friends, and he is living within us!" (Romans 5:8-10).

You also affirm that your salvation comes through grace, that you receive it without cost: "Because of his kindness, you have been saved through trusting Christ. And even trusting is not of yourselves; it too is a gift from God. Salvation is not a reward for the good we have done, so none of us can take any credit for it" (Ephesians 2:8, 9).

"Saved by grace" means that the payment for anyone's salvation is made entirely by God's power through Jesus' sinless life, sacrificial death, and mighty resurrection. Our participation in receiving God's gift of salvation is accomplished entirely through our trusting in Christ and relying completely on what he has done.

As you come to water baptism, both the foundation for your rejoicing and the hope for your future are based upon these steadfast truths about your salvation. You are affirming God's goodness and grace to you through the sacrifice of his Son, Jesus.

No wonder we sing, praise, and worship God when we come to be baptized. And no wonder those sharing that moment with you are so happy about what is happening!

# CHAPTER SIX
# THE FAMILY'S FREEDOM

One of the most beautiful words in our language is *freedom*. Although human systems often corrupt the meaning of this word, the Bible describes a pure freedom that releases us from sin's guilt and power and opens the prison gates of our souls, delivering us into a new day of Christ's rule in our lives.

Being born into the family of God involves the privileges of choice, and—as a new disciple of the Lord Jesus—responsible choices begin with your obedience to his command to be baptized in water. When you obey this command two things take place: (1) You verify or ratify your decision to receive Jesus as your Savior, and (2) you make way for his further work in your life as he breaks the chains binding you to the past and he fills you with his love and power.

## WATER BAPTISM: A RATIFICATION

To ratify something is to confirm or to formally establish it by indicating approval. For example, ratification is what you as a citizen of a community do when you enter a yes vote on a proposed law.

In coming for water baptism, you are taking a specific action that says you agree with, or ratify, God's Word—his Law. You agree that you are dependent upon his Son, the only Savior from sin. "For God loved the world so much that he gave his only Son so that anyone who believes in him shall not perish but have eternal life" (John 3:16).

You are saying that you believe in Christ's promise to forgive and transform you. "When someone becomes a Christian he becomes a brand new person inside. He is not the same anymore. A new life has begun!" (2 Corinthians 5:17).

You commit yourself to his Word and his way in your life. "The one who obeys me is the one who loves me; and because he loves me, my Father will love him; and I will too, and I will reveal myself to him" (John 14:21).

You are open to God's Holy Spirit filling you with his power and love. "Each one of you must turn from sin, return to God, and be baptized in the name of Jesus Christ for the forgiveness of your sins; then you also shall receive this gift, the Holy Spirit" (Acts 2:38).

So the following statements summarize what it

means to "believe and be baptized": I am ratifying God's command to bring my life in line with his spiritual laws and I recognize the reality of the invisible spirit realm of his working and power. Through faith I take seriously what I can't see with my eyes, because I believe in the reality of what God has said in his Word. I acknowledge my submission to the Kingdom of God—I surrender to his appointed King, Jesus the Lord, and am determined to try to walk according to his Word, the Bible. I affirm Christ's promise to give me the Holy Spirit to fill and overflow my life with his power, for this gives me assurance that I can live my faith daily, in a practical way.

## WATER BAPTISM: DEATH AND RESURRECTION

One of the most powerful facts about water baptism is that it establishes a definite point at which we bid farewell to the way of life we have led outside of Jesus Christ. The Bible teaches that it is a burial of our "old man"—the sinning, selfishness, and carnality of the past.

> Sin's power over us was broken when we became Christians and were baptized to become a part of Jesus Christ; through his death the power of your sinful nature was shattered. Your old sin-loving nature was buried with him by baptism when he died, and when God the Father, with glorious power, brought him back to life again, you

> were given his wonderful new life to enjoy.
> For you have become a part of him, and so
> you died with him, so to speak, when he
> died; and now you share his new life, and
> shall rise as he did. (Romans 6:3-5)

Besides burial, another comparison is made to
help us understand moving into the practical
dimension of living daily under the Lordship of
Jesus Christ. *Circumcision* is the Old Testament
rite by which every male was pledged to God. It
also is applied in a spiritual sense to every New
Testament believer at the time of water baptism:
"When you came to Christ he set you free from
your evil desires, not by a bodily operation of
circumcision but by a spiritual operation, the
baptism of your souls. For in baptism you see
how your old, evil nature died with him and was
buried with him; and then you came up out of
death with him into a new life because you
trusted the Word of the mighty God who raised
Christ from the dead" (Colossians 2:11, 12). In
other words, in Christ a spiritual form of circumcision is made when believers are buried with
him in water baptism. The cutting away of past
connection with sinning frees believers to believe in God's ability to work Christ's resurrection
power in their daily living.

Just as the burial and the circumcision being
taught here are illustrations, so the resurrection
referred to is not the resurrection that will occur
in the future at Christ's second coming. It is right

now! It is God's way of saying to us, "If I could raise my Son from the dead after he died for your sins, I can also pour the power of his victorious life into you now, so that you can grow in victory over sinning and failure!"

This is a thrilling promise—one we must embrace in simple faith. Believe that Jesus will make it real in your daily experience; you do not need to be ruled by sin anymore! That is not to say that you will never sin again for the rest of your life, but that the power of Christ's life within you will lead you to a progressive victory over past patterns of sin.

Let your baptism in water be a landmark moment in your life. Drive a stake there! Raise a monument!

Determine that, from that moment, you will grow in experiencing Jesus' progressive triumph in your daily conduct, conversation, business, and relationships. God's love and forgiveness are ever-ready resources if you fail, but let none of us ever presume to use that graciousness as a license for sin or self-indulgence. God has made a way of liberty from sin's bondage, and your water baptism is designed by him to be your entrance into an ongoing discovery of that victory.

## A DELIVERANCE

I was once beside a couple who had come, along with several others, into the baptistry for baptism. I had never met the couple, but knew from the baptismal cards they handed me that they were married.

As I looked into their faces, the Holy Spirit whispered to my heart: "They have deep marital problems because of immoral acts prior to their marriage. Speak to them. I'll free them tonight as they are baptized."

To avoid embarrassing them in front of the others who also were being baptized, I drew them aside as the congregation sang a song of worship.

"Please don't feel embarrassed," I told them quietly. "What I have to share is not in condemnation, but because Jesus wants these baptismal waters to be waters of deliverance for you both.

"I must be direct: The Holy Spirit has just shown me two things about you. First, you had sexual intercourse together before you were married, didn't you?"

They looked at each other a moment, and then back at me. They recognized I was not judging them, but that I was seeking to help them.

"Yes," they said together.

"Secondly, you are having real stress in your marriage—and are especially hindered in your sexual relationship."

"Right," they said, nodding.

"Listen," I continued, "the Holy Spirit has not revealed this to shame you, but to show he is ready to free you from the bonds of past sin; a bondage you couldn't break because you didn't even know it was related to sins committed before you knew Jesus. So, right now, confess to him that you specifically reject your past way of thought that excused such action. If you can do that, you will experience a real deliverance as you are baptized tonight."

We prayed briefly and then rejoined the others and proceeded with baptism.

Several days later I received a beautiful letter from this couple:

> Dear Pastor Jack,
>
> There are hardly words to describe the change we have realized in our lives and in our marriage. Invisible chains have been broken and freeing life and joy have entered our home and our relationship. Thank you for your sensitivity to the Holy Spirit.
>
> We have been born again for six months, but were somehow hesitant to be baptized. The forgiveness we found with our salvation was no less real, but we did wonder why we were so unable to "get it all together."
>
> Now Jesus has done it! Obedience to baptism coupled with the Holy Spirit's presence and power has untangled the past and opened the door to a new kind of life and marriage for us. Praise his name!

This true story is not surprising because it is based on a biblical truth that is dramatically demonstrated in the Old Testament story of Israel's escape from Egypt. The significance of that episode is taught in the New Testament when, speaking of Israel's escape through the parted waters of the Red Sea, Paul says in 1 Corinthians 10:2 that this "might be called their 'baptism' . . . as followers of Moses." In other words, Moses leading the Israelites out of slavery to the Egyptians is a picture of Christ leading us out of slavery to sin. Moses was God's instrument to prophetically portray two major factors in the salvation Jesus brings:

1. *We are saved from judgment.* Just as the blood of the Passover lamb kept the children of Israel from death (see Exodus 12:21-23), so the blood of Jesus Christ is the basis for our salvation from judgment (see John 1:29; 1 Peter 1:18, 19).

2. *We are delivered from oppression.* Just as the Israelites' passage through the Red Sea accomplished both their entry into a new time and place and the destruction of their former oppressors (see Exodus 14:19-31), so our water baptism is a moment when we enter into a new level of commitment and when any cords of spiritual bondage to the past may be severed (see Colossians 2:12-15).

Studying this lesson in God's Word, it is clear to see that our introduction to Christ involves a double deliverance—deliverance from sin's judgment and from its bondage.

As you are baptized, bring to the Lord Jesus any hateful habit or carnal bondage you may have in attitude, relationship, or circumstance. Let anything that is residue from the past—ties that still seem to link you to old slavery, defeat, or failure—be presented to him for deliverance. For he is the One who said: "The Spirit of the Lord is upon me; he has appointed me to preach Good News to the poor; he has sent me to heal the brokenhearted and to announce that captives shall be released and the blind shall see, that the downtrodden shall be freed from their oppressors" (Luke 4:18).

Come in faith, meeting Jesus at the waters of baptism, and allow him to be your Deliverer. He is able, for "no other God can save in this way!" (Daniel 3:29).

# CHAPTER SEVEN
# THE FAMILY'S FOCUS

Those who have been born into the family of God want to do the right thing. It isn't a matter of trying to earn God's favor by doing so, for he has already shown us his favor by loving us and giving us forgiveness and acceptance in Christ. But it is a fact that when his Holy Spirit comes to dwell in a person's life, a new focus occurs.

The Bible uses the word *righteousness* to describe this focus. And wanting to do righteous things requires much more than doing religious things—acting pious or trying to outdo others in good deeds. This desire for righteousness is another reason that being baptized as soon as possible after you have made your personal decision to follow Christ is so important. Your obedience in baptism will open the way toward insight and power for walking in the way that your life's new focus is calling you.

The best place to see how this focus and your water baptism connect is to take a look at the biblical record of Jesus' own baptism experience. The report begins in the New Testament, in Matthew 3. John, whose commission from God was to call people to repent and prepare for the coming of the Messiah, was baptizing those who responded to his preaching. Then one day, a different One came to the Jordan River where John was preaching. Here was a sinless man— One whom John would identify to the crowds as "the Lamb of God, who takes away the sin of the world!" (John 1:29). The Bible tells us of John's response to Jesus' coming for baptism:

> Then Jesus went from Galilee to the Jordan River to be baptized there by John. John didn't want to do it.
>
> "This isn't proper," he said. "I am the one who needs to be baptized by you."
>
> But Jesus said, "Please do it, for I must do all that is right." So then John baptized him.
>
> After his baptism, as soon as Jesus came up out of the water, the heavens were opened to him and he saw the Spirit of God coming down in the form of a dove. And a voice from heaven said, "This is my beloved Son, and I am wonderfully pleased with him." (Matthew 3:13-17)

Take note of Jesus' words: "I must [by means of water baptism] do all that is right" (v. 15). He clearly did not mean water baptism would make him holier, for he was without sin. And in the same way, he does not call you to be baptized in order to make you more worthy. It is your faith in Christ as your Savior that establishes your right standing before God; it is through faith you are forgiven, cleansed, reborn, made righteous, and accepted. Yet Jesus said that something more needed to be done to do all that is right; God's plan for man's salvation had more to it than simply restoring man to a position of holiness in God's sight.

We can see exactly what Jesus meant by looking at what occurred when he was baptized. Three distinct things happened, and in each there is a truth for you to grasp as you are baptized.

1. *"The heavens were opened to him."* This doesn't mean the sky opened up, but that the invisible spiritual realm became more vivid to Christ, giving him spiritual insight for the purpose of ministering to others.

2. *"The Spirit of God coming down in the form of a dove."* This doesn't mean a bird sat on Jesus' head or shoulder, but that the gentle yet powerful presence of God settled upon him like a mantle of love, giving him increased spiritual energy for the purpose of serving others.

3. *"A voice from heaven said, 'This is my beloved Son, and I am wonderfully pleased with him.'"* This clear statement indicated the Father's

pleasure with his Son's sinlessness during the thirty years leading to this moment and declared that Christ had God's full authority to represent him to mankind.

All three of these things that Jesus received at his baptism—discernment, dynamic, and designation—were for the practical purposes of life and service. None of them are mysterious. Therefore, we can see their practicality for our own lives. And we can see that, in calling us to follow him in water baptism, Jesus is inviting us to share the full dimensions of his own baptism experience!

Jesus wants to give you *discernment* because he wants his followers to "see" spiritual things, to perceive the reality of the spiritual realm. He isn't anxious for you to become weird or mystical, but he does want you to understand that the invisible spirit realm is no less real than the tangible world of your five physical senses (see 1 Corinthians 2:10-14).

The *dynamic* you will receive through baptism is the fullness of the Holy Spirit in your life. Christ's conception was through the Spirit, but through his baptism he was anointed for his ministry. In the same way, when you were born again you were birthed by the Spirit, but at your baptism Jesus wants to provide you with a fuller sense of the Holy Spirit's power and presence in your life.

The *designation* of baptism that Christ desires for you is the Father's seal, a clear statement that you are his; that he is lovingly pleased with you and that he is authorizing you to represent him.

These are the reasons Jesus wants "all that is right" to be fulfilled in each of us, for this rightness or righteousness refers to God's ability to do things right. Just as it is entirely God's power that saves us and makes us right with him, it is also entirely his power that will enable us to serve him rightly.

In the light of these truths, you can see why water baptism is so very important in God's order for verifying your discipleship under his Lordship. Jesus is emphatic about this.

Being baptized is not a matter of church activity or religious formalism, but one of obedience to our Master. While his command is not made in the spirit of a dictator, it does reflect his deep desire and full intention that we receive all he has planned for us. So we can understand the urgency of coming to be baptized. Jesus has commanded us; let us be quick to obey. Just as the Ethiopian official said to Philip as soon as he could find a place to be baptized, "Look! Water! Why can't I be baptized?" (Acts 8:36). He wanted to be obedient and declarative about his commitment to Jesus Christ—and he was.

Be like that. It's a scriptural and powerful attitude! Come as a child—a newborn child of the Most High God. Come as a forgiven sinner cleansed through the blood of Jesus. Come as a family member, ready to receive the Holy Spirit's fullest blessing for you!

Come to the waters of baptism and meet

Jesus there to receive the special encounter he has planned for you. (If you have further questions regarding water baptism, please turn to the question and answer section on page 58 of this booklet.)

# CHAPTER EIGHT
# THE FAMILY'S FULLNESS

God's Word clearly establishes the sequence for our obedient response to God as newborn members of his family. First, we must repent, receive Jesus as our Savior, and be forgiven of sin. Second, we are called to water baptism. Third, we are urged to receive the Holy Spirit, and through this to be filled with Christ's life, love, and power.

An example of this threefold reality (being forgiven, baptized, and then filled with power) can be seen in the scriptural account of the birth of the Church at Pentecost (see Acts 2:1-29). The instructions for a fullhearted, right response to God are found in Acts 2:38: "Each one of you must turn from sin, return to God, and be baptized in the name of Jesus Christ for the forgiveness of your sins; then you also shall receive this gift, the Holy Spirit."

This is an invitation to an experience Jesus wants for all of us—receiving his gift of the Holy Spirit, who will give us divine power for living and serving God daily (see John 20:21, 22; Acts 1:8). We aren't called to run a spiritual survival course, as though our only prospect is to struggle through our earthly lives until we get to heaven someday. Jesus wants to give us the full resources of the Holy Spirit now to bring us both joy and ability in our daily lives. He wants us to influence the world around us in loving, meaningful ways—and we can do this through the power of the Holy Spirit (see Luke 24:49; Acts 1:5; 2:1-4).

NEW TESTAMENT PRAYER
As you read the Book of Acts, you will find that receiving and living in the Holy Spirit's power was the very heartbeat of the early believers' lives. All newborn believers were introduced to receiving the fullness of the Holy Spirit (see Acts 8:14-17; 19:1-6). Family members would gather in prayer and praise, reverently placing their hands on the head of the new believer as he invited Jesus to fill him with his life and love. And then as now, God answered his childrens' prayers: They were filled with the Spirit of God's love.

The promise of that same experience is ours today (see Romans 5:5). And the same power those early believers received—to heal the sick and strengthen weak people with the faith that

Christ was working in their lives—is available for us today (see John 20:21, 22).

The Bible further notes that through the Spirit these early believers enjoyed a broadened dimension of prayer, praise, and communication with the heavenly Father (see Acts 2:4, 11; 1 Corinthians 14:2). Jesus prophesied that this would happen, and that, by his fullness in their lives, they would triumph over satanic powers while lovingly serving those in need (see Mark 16:17, 18).

Biblical examples make it clear that we should encourage every believer to receive the fullness of the Holy Spirit just as those people who lived in Bible times did. Such an experience is available to any believer at any time, right up to the present day. This promise has been available since Pentecost, the day the Church was born (see Acts 2).

At Pentecost, after Peter had preached and explained the phenomenal things that had occurred with the outpouring of the Holy Spirit upon the newly born Church, earnest inquirers asked, "What should we do?" Peter answered with this command: "Each one of you must turn from sin, return to God, and be baptized in the name of Jesus Christ for the forgiveness of your sins." Then he declared the promise, "You also shall receive this gift, the Holy Spirit" (Acts 2:37, 38).

Look at this! The Church is only hours old, and already a second generation of newborn believers

is being ushered in! True to Christ's desire for his
Church, these believers were being promised the
same outpouring of the Spirit upon their lives
that Jesus had received and the same fullness
that had been given to those whom they had just
seen and heard coming from the upper room of
Pentecost (see Acts 1:12–2:36).

Listen to Peter encourage them to expect the
Holy Spirit to fill them: "The promise is to you
and your children" (Acts 2:39, NKJV). He is saying,
"You can have what we've tasted, for just as Jesus
has sent us the same Spirit that rested on him
with blessing and power, so you can have the
same resource of God's fullness!" And that
message from the Word of God awakens faith
today.

Notice what Peter went on to say: ". . . and to
all who are afar off, as many as the Lord our God
will call." The words "all who are afar off"
include you and me and anyone else who answers
the call of God to repentance and faith in his
Son, Jesus Christ, and to receive of the love, life,
and power of his Holy Spirit.

Many years later in the city of Ephesus, Paul
offered the same encouragement that Peter gave.
So we can see that the promise of the Holy
Spirit's power was not—is not—confined to any
single period.

Paul encountered a group of sincere believers
who had not yet come to a full understanding of
the scope of life Jesus brings to us (see Acts
19:1-6). He inquired of them, "Did you receive the

Holy Spirit when you believed?" (Acts 19:2).
Their response, "We don't know what you mean.
What is the Holy Spirit?" indicated that they did
not know the dynamic possibilities available to
them through the Lord Jesus. So Paul instructed
them, baptized them, and then encouraged them
to receive the full measure of the Holy Spirit.
They did as he told them, and they beautifully
experienced the same joy as those on that first
day at Pentecost years before: a God-given
language of praise flowed forth from their
freshly filled hearts.

Later, in a letter to these same people (the
Ephesians), Paul refers to this occasion of their
receiving the Holy Spirit, and says, "All you
others, too, who heard the Good News about
how to be saved and trusted Christ, were marked
as belonging to the Holy Spirit" (Ephesians 1:13).
Three facts about this Scripture stand out: The
"marking" or "sealing" of these believers came
after they had already believed in Christ; it
occurred in conjunction with their baptism in
water; and it was experienced as they received
the fullness of the Holy Spirit. These Scriptures
reveal a timeless truth that invites us to our own
personal experience of the same: Jesus wants to
seal each of us with the Holy Spirit, and to fill
our lives with his love and power.

Seals have always been instruments by which
authority has been conferred, documents authen-
ticated, and clear ownership marked. And so it is
from the moment of your new birth, in the waters

of baptism, and through being filled with his Spirit that Jesus Christ wants you to bear the imprint of his own person and purpose on your life. As one hymnwriter put it:

> Oh, to be like Thee!
> Oh, to be like Thee,
> Blessed Redeemer, pure as Thou art!
> Come in Thy sweetness; come in Thy
>     fullness,
> Stamp Thine own image deep on my heart.

> *Thomas O. Chisholm*

As you have opened your heart to the Savior, and as you have obeyed him and been baptized, now ask him to fill you with the Holy Spirit.

## BEING FILLED WITH THE SPIRIT

Jesus said that those who long for God's fullness shall receive it (see Matthew 5:6; Luke 11:11-13). When you obey his command to repent and be baptized in water, you have scriptural reason to believe Christ's promise that "you shall also receive this gift, the Holy Spirit" (Acts 2:38). Come to Jesus and ask him to fill you with the Holy Spirit, just as he did those believers at the beginning. Ask fellow believers to pray with you, praising God together. Praise opens a place in our souls for the Holy Spirit to overflow. God created us to praise him, and his Word promises us blessing when we do so. So let your praise ring out!

Move into the intimacy, blessing, and joy of the fullness the Lord Jesus has promised to each of us in the Father's family.

# CHAPTER NINE
# THE FAMILY'S FUTURE

There is one promise in the Bible that stirs the heart of every one who has come to know the Lord Jesus Christ as Savior. Christ gave this promise himself:

> Let not your heart be troubled. You are trusting God, now trust in me. There are many homes up there where my Father lives, and I am going to prepare them for your coming. When everything is ready, then I will come and get you, so that you can always be with me where I am. (John 14:1-4)

Jesus' promise is that he is coming back again! He promises all of us that even if death comes to us before his return from heaven, we shall all be with the Lord forever:

> I can tell you this directly from the Lord: that we who are still living when the Lord returns will not rise to meet him ahead of those who are in their graves. For the Lord himself will come down from heaven with a mighty shout and with the soul-stirring cry of the archangel and the great trumpet-call of God. And the believers who are dead will be the first to rise to meet the Lord. Then we who are still alive and remain on the earth will be caught up with them in the clouds to meet the Lord in the air and re- main with him forever. So comfort and encourage each other with this news.
> (1 Thessalonians 4:15-18)

When such passages as this, which fill the New Testament, are coupled with the biblical proph- ecies that we can already see being fulfilled around us, they serve as strong evidence that we are living in a time when our hearts should be expectant and ready for Christ's return.

This—the return of our Savior—has always been the wholesome hope and joyous anticipa- tion of every believer. Our lives are not pointless, but directed toward a lifetime goal of serving Christ and an eternal goal of being with him forever.

In reality, we could be called the Father's

"forever family"! A family into which, when you picked up this book and began reading, you had only recently been born. Now that you've progressed through these few pages, I'm hoping you have not only read them but taken the steps they teach—for the guidelines are God's, not mine.

As a summary, let me give you something of a checklist to see if, as a newborn, you are giving attention to the basics that ensure a strong start and healthy growth in your life with Christ:

1. Write down the date you received Jesus as your Savior:

_____

2. Remember the seven great things that God has already accomplished for you as a result of your being born again (see pages 11 and 12).

3. Be sure to regularly feed on the Word of God, beginning with the Gospel of John provided at the end of this booklet.

4. Don't let anything hinder your regular fellowship with the brothers and sisters you find in the church you make your home.

5. Write down the date of your water baptism:

_____

6. Write down when you asked the Lord Jesus to fill you with the Holy Spirit:

_____

7. Stop with me right now and let's join in prayerful praise, rejoicing in the Lord Jesus Christ who has saved us, filled us with his Holy Spirit, and promised to come again to take us to live with him forever!

I'll see you then!

# CHAPTER TEN

# QUESTIONS ABOUT WATER BAPTISM

Through my years of pastoral ministry, I have been asked many common questions related to water baptism. These questions, and the answers I and my pastoral staff have found for them, are listed here in the hope that they will help you in your study.

**What should I do if I was baptized as an infant or at some other early point in my life? Should I be baptized again as an adult?**

This question requires a sensitive answer because it is a common experience of many sincere and earnest believers. The key to finding a clear answer is to establish why the earlier baptism took place and what it meant. This will vary widely from family to family.

First, if your parents had you christened or

baptized when you were a baby, you should be thankful. Whatever degree of understanding they may or may not have had, two things are very clear: They cared about your spiritual well-being, and God heard their heart-prayer.

I say "God heard" because here you are, someone who has responded to his Son, Jesus Christ, and received him as your own Savior. Regardless of your parents' understanding, the fact that you have become spiritually sensitized to God's desire and purpose for you is evidence of his faithfulness in honoring your parents' or guardians' act.

For you to be baptized now of your own choice—as an action of your will—is not inconsistent with the loving interest these people showed you as a child. Obeying Christ's command to be baptized as you acknowledge him as your own Lord and Savior is not a rejection of the love or sincerity that prompted your earlier baptism. But failing to be baptized on the supposition that your parents' or guardians' action substitutes for your obedience is to misunderstand the Word of God.

Acts 2:38 says, "Turn from sin . . . and be baptized." This indicates a sequence: the decision to turn away from your sins to Christ is *followed* by baptism, not preceded by it.

The same principle can also apply to earlier baptism that was initiated on your part. A woman said, "When I was a teenager, I attended a summer youth camp where I was baptized. However,

I didn't fully understand the reality of Christ as I do now." A young man said, "I was at the beach with some friends whose church was holding a baptism service there. I was moved by what I saw and, when asked if I also wanted to be baptized, I consented. I was sincere, but I didn't really understand baptism as I do now that I have met Jesus in a more personal way."

Each of these people were baptized twice, but their baptism as an understanding believer was the first instance of their own true surrender to Christ as Lord and Savior. And their second baptism is scriptural, not because it rescinds or denies any meaning an earlier experience may have held, but because these people recognize that while they had been open to God at their first baptism, a full-hearted receiving of Christ as Savior was outside their understanding at that time.

So, since baptism is meant to follow a fully understood repentance that results in faith being placed in what Jesus alone has done to save us, any earlier baptisms, however sincere, are not considered the baptism to which Jesus calls us as his disciples (see Matthew 28:19, 20).

**Hebrews 6:2 specifically states that the fundamentals of New Testament teaching involve a "doctrine of baptisms." What is this and why is "baptism" plural in this passage?**

Baptism is plural in this verse because the

early church taught, as we should today, a threefold baptism of the believer. The three baptisms are baptism into the body, or family, of Jesus Christ; baptism in water through faith in Jesus Christ; and baptism in the Holy Spirit by Jesus Christ.

Each baptism is distinct from the others, and requires a decision on the part of the believer. And yet, through Christ, the three baptisms become one; thus no contradiction exists between the "baptisms" of Hebrews 6:2 and the "one baptism" described in Ephesians 4:5.

The first baptism, into the body of Christ, is done by the Holy Spirit. It is he who draws us to Christ, who makes us new through faith in Christ as we respond and repent, and who then places or baptizes us into Christ's body. This is how we became a redeemed part of the living Church. Through our "immersion" in Christ we are united as one with our Lord and his people.

The second baptism, water baptism, is done by the pastoral or spiritual leadership of the church. As we've already discussed, this baptism is required according to biblical commandment and example (see Acts 2:41; 8:12; 9:18; 10:48; 16:33; 18:8). And the potential of the real spiritual power promised us with baptism in water makes this baptism far more than a ritual, and certainly not optional.

The third baptism, in the Holy Spirit, is done by Jesus himself. "Jesus is the one who baptizes with the Holy Spirit" (John 1:33); "The Father

gave him the authority to send the Holy Spirit—
with the results you are seeing and hearing
today" (see Acts 2:33). Both Jesus and John
called this the baptism in the Holy Spirit (see
Acts 1:5). And just as Jesus called his disciples to
receive this power, he calls each of us to receive
it today (see John 20:22; Luke 24:49).

## Why do we baptize by immersion?

Immersion—placing the entire body under the
water when baptizing—is our practice because it
is the most natural meaning of the Greek verbs
*bapto/baptizo,* which are used in the New Testament for *baptism.* According to Gerhard Kittel's
*Theological Dictionary of the New Testament,*
this verb was regularly used in ways that unmis-
takably indicate complete, total immersion.
Examples of how *bapto* was used include a
reference to a sunken ship (completely under
water) and an article of clothing being dyed
another color (completely dipped so the whole
garment is dyed). Furthermore, the picture the
Bible gives us is that of baptism paralleling
burial; in which, of course, a body is completely
covered (see Romans 6:3-5).

## What other forms of water baptism are used in churches? How do you feel about them?

Other forms of baptism are sprinkling and
effusion (which is done by pouring water over
the candidate's head). These are both practiced
widely and with varying degrees of insistence.

Some churches even allow a candidate to select which form he prefers. And, where infant baptism is practiced, it is easy to see how forms other than immersion evolved.

While I am convinced that the significance of immersion is great and that it ought to be the method employed, I will not disapprove of those who observe another form of water baptism. The method of baptism is not nearly so important as whether or not the candidate has truly received Christ and is truly acknowledging Christ's lordship in his life. Members of our pastoral team have, in fact, sprinkled deathbed or invalid cases when they requested baptism. But we have also, at their request and with the physicians' permission, brought the dying or the invalid to a place of immersion, and carried them into the baptistry or pool.

## What is "baptismal regeneration"?

Baptismal regeneration is a teaching based on the belief that the moment a person is baptized in water he or she is actually "born again" (regenerated) or "saved." This belief is argued from such passages as Mark 16:16 and John 3:5, but it finds little support when these texts are balanced with the whole of Scripture on the subject.

Baptismal regeneration is a belief sometimes held by those who baptize infants or by those who are concerned that someone be baptized before they die, as though the act of baptism could accomplish salvation.

We refuse to take an argumentative position on the matter of baptismal regeneration, although the general application of the practice would seem to blur the requirements of repentance and faith for salvation. Many who observe these practices genuinely believe that the Holy Spirit will fulfill the promise they feel they are responding to in being baptized. But, unfortunately, there are also people who have been led to believe that their baptism established their eternal salvation before God, which is untrue.

There are people who were baptized as infants and, having been raised to walk in the way of the Lord from their childhood, believe that early baptism had something to do with their life of faith. Among these, one often meets those who cannot pinpoint a certain moment or time when they "accepted Christ," but who have always "loved the Lord," or "believed in Jesus." And who can deny the possibility that the roots of their faith were established at their baptism as an infant or as a very small child?

Sometimes such a person will ask, "Should I be baptized as an adult?" My answer is always the same. First, I offer the question: "Why do you ask?" Second, I give this directive: "Ask Jesus to tell you—he's your Lord."

And their response is usually the same: they asked because they had inner doubts about the validity of the earlier baptism. With prayer, they generally discover that the Holy Spirit was prompting them to obey God's command to turn from sin and be baptized, and to do so in the actions and the sequence given in God's Word.

### What about those who fear a baptism is not valid unless done specifically "in Jesus' name"?

Every ordinance of God is touched by fears that evolve from sincere traditionalism that lacks sufficient scriptural support. This particular question is generally asked by one of two groups: People who reduce the meaning of such Scriptures as Acts 2:38 and 10:48 to legal formulas, or people who insist on the formula "in Jesus' name" because they do not believe in the Holy Trinity of the Godhead.

The first group is answered by Jesus' own words in John 6:63, in which he states that any truth is best understood and lived out in the spirit of that truth. Paul said the same thing in 2 Corinthians 3:6, and warned against the death-dealing power of spiritless literalism.

The second group declares that Jesus' directions to baptize "in the name of the Father and of the Son and of the Holy Spirit" are polytheistic, practicing the worship of many gods. But Jesus made clear the unity of the Godhead (see Mark 12:29), and he declared the truth of the Trinity in his words in Matthew 28:19. (Note that these words are Jesus' only specific instructions as to how and in what way a baptismal declaration should be made. That points rather conclusively to the rightness of this statement which has been used by believers through the centuries.)

It is helpful to understand that the scriptural meaning of "in the name of" means "under the authority, according to the merits, or consistent with the character of." When a person confesses Jesus Christ as his Savior and is baptized according to the direct commandment of Jesus—"in the name of the Father and of the Son and of the Holy Spirit,"—he is accurately acting on the concept involved when one says "in the name of." And he is doing what Jesus said, the way Jesus said to do it.

## Should a person who has already been baptized after a mature, conscious decision for Christ ever be rebaptized?

There is nothing to be said against such a practice, although there is no need to encourage it. There are situations that have prompted people to be baptized again. For example, people have requested—and received—a second baptism (1) after having returned from an extended season of disobedience to Jesus; (2) upon recognizing a dimension of faith in or commitment to Christ that seemed to call for them to respond with an outward expression of a new stance toward life; (3) when a couple has been reconciled or one of the two came to Christ at a later date and they both felt the desire to be baptized together.

Resolving this issue is not done in a law or a proof text, but in the heart of the disciple. Being rebaptized may be a fulfilling experience if the Holy Spirit is indeed doing something special in your heart.

But rebaptism on the basis of superstition or religious gamesmanship is always fruitless and sometimes destructive.

## Who may baptize a person in water?

Every case of water baptism in the Bible has this common denominator: it is performed under authority. Both the person who does the baptizing of believers, and the reasons for and occurrences of baptism are considered important. Jesus directed his disciples to baptize; John says he baptized because he was commissioned to do so; and the Scriptures show apostles, evangelists, and elders baptizing. (The biblical definition of "elders" indicates people of appointed, recognized leadership who are of consistent character and faithfulness in a local church.)

At times there have been cases of sincere but mistaken practices in water baptism, where people baptize on an impulse, or "baptize each other," or blithely suggest that "any believer can do it." While I do not wish to insist on hierarchical control of water baptism, I do want to make this general observation: Jesus wants the power of the Holy Spirit to be attendant at and manifest in water baptism. This will most likely happen as intended when experienced, mature leadership in the body of Christ perform the baptism.

**Is there some special way I can be baptized that doesn't require my head being placed under the water? I have a terrible fear of that.**

To some, this may seem a peculiar or even humorous question, but it is a very serious concern for many. (Our pastoral staff has encountered this on a number of occasions.)

Unless there is a medical reason you should not be immersed, we strongly encourage you to allow sensitive and Spirit-filled elders or pastors to baptize you by immersion. Remember that we have discussed the waters of baptism as a frequent point of deliverance. This would be a case where I would expect to see a person not only graciously led to the pathway of obedience in being immersed, but I would expect them to be delivered from "bondage to fear" as well (see Romans 8:15).

The Bible says, "God has not given us a spirit of fear, but of power and of love and of a sound mind" (2 Timothy 1:7, NKJV), and "There is no fear in love; but perfect love casts out fear, because fear involves torment. But he who fears has not been made perfect in love" (1 John 4:18, NKJV). These two verses teach us the source of such binding fears and the method of release from those fears. The source is "a spirit." We are not dealing with a mere psychological hang-up, but with a point of spiritual oppression. The method of release can be the patient and loving ministering of both water baptism and deliverance.

I would propose that gentleness and understanding be joined to authoritative prayer and the declaration of dominion over that fear-spirit through invoking the power of Jesus' name and inviting the presence of the Holy Spirit. Victory and release will be given to those who ask in obedience and faith!

**I would prefer a private water baptism since I feel awkward, frightened, or embarrassed in front of crowds or large groups. Is this all right?**

The Bible clearly allows for baptisms at which no significant number of people are present, so private baptism is not in violation of the Word of God (see Acts 8:36-38; 16:25-34).

However, as a general rule, I would recommend that whoever desires private baptism be counseled to see if personal ministry, such as release from fear of water, is needed. Both fear and pride have subtle ways of intruding themselves upon sincere believers, and every spirit that diminishes the dominion of Christ and his glory in our lives should be confronted lovingly and authoritatively.

# THE GOSPEL OF JOHN

**1** Before anything else existed, there was Christ, with God. He has always been alive and is himself God. ³ He created everything there is—nothing exists that he didn't make. ⁴ Eternal life is in him, and this life gives light to all mankind. ⁵ His life is the light that shines through the darkness—and the darkness can never extinguish it.

⁶,⁷ God sent John the Baptist as a witness to the fact that Jesus Christ is the true Light. ⁸ John himself was not the Light; he was only a witness to identify it.

⁹ Later on, the one who is the true Light arrived to shine on everyone coming into the world.

¹⁰ But although he made the world, the world didn't recognize him when he came. ¹¹,¹² Even in his own land and among his own people, the Jews, he was not accepted. Only a few would

welcome and receive him. But to all who received
him, he gave the right to become children of God.
All they needed to do was to trust him to save
them. [13] All those who believe this are reborn!—
not a physical rebirth resulting from human
passion or plan—but from the will of God.

[14] And Christ became a human being and lived
here on earth among us and was full of loving
forgiveness and truth. And some of us have seen
his glory—the glory of the only Son of the
heavenly Father!

[15] John pointed him out to the people, telling
the crowds, "This is the one I was talking about
when I said, 'Someone is coming who is greater
by far than I am—for he existed long before I
did!' " [16] We have all benefited from the rich
blessings he brought to us—blessing upon
blessing heaped upon us! [17] For Moses gave us
only the Law with its rigid demands and
merciless justice, while Jesus Christ brought us
loving forgiveness as well. [18] No one has ever
actually seen God, but, of course, his only Son
has, for he is the companion of the Father and
has told us all about him.

[19] The Jewish leaders sent priests and assistant
priests from Jerusalem to ask John whether he
claimed to be the Messiah.

[20] He denied it flatly. "I am not the Christ," he
said.

[21] "Well then, who are you?" they asked. "Are
you Elijah?"

"No," he replied.

"Are you the Prophet?"

"No."

[22] "Then who are you? Tell us, so we can give

an answer to those who sent us. What do you have to say for yourself?"

23 He replied, "I am a voice from the barren wilderness, shouting as Isaiah prophesied, 'Get ready for the coming of the Lord!' "

24, 25 Then those who were sent by the Pharisees asked him, "If you aren't the Messiah or Elijah or the Prophet, what right do you have to baptize?"

26 John told them, "I merely baptize with water, but right here in the crowd is someone you have never met, 27 who will soon begin his ministry among you, and I am not even fit to be his slave."

28 This incident took place at Bethany, a village on the other side of the Jordan River where John was baptizing.

29 The next day John saw Jesus coming toward him and said, "Look! There is the Lamb of God who takes away the world's sin! 30 He is the one I was talking about when I said, 'Soon a man far greater than I am is coming, who existed long before me!' 31 I didn't know he was the one, but I am here baptizing with water in order to point him out to the nation of Israel."

32 Then John told about seeing the Holy Spirit in the form of a dove descending from heaven and resting upon Jesus.

33 "I didn't know he was the one," John said again, "but at the time God sent me to baptize he told me, 'When you see the Holy Spirit descending and resting upon someone—he is the one you are looking for. He is the one who baptizes with the Holy Spirit.' 34 I saw it happen to this man, and I therefore testify that he is the Son of God."

<sup>35</sup> The following day as John was standing with two of his disciples, <sup>36</sup> Jesus walked by. John looked at him intently and then declared, "See! There is the Lamb of God!"

<sup>37</sup> Then John's two disciples turned and followed Jesus.

<sup>38</sup> Jesus looked around and saw them following. "What do you want?" he asked them.

"Sir," they replied, "where do you live?"

<sup>39</sup> "Come and see," he said. So they went with him to the place where he was staying and were with him from about four o'clock that afternoon until the evening. <sup>40</sup> (One of these men was Andrew, Simon Peter's brother.)

<sup>41</sup> Andrew then went to find his brother Peter and told him, "We have found the Messiah!" <sup>42</sup> And he brought Peter to meet Jesus.

Jesus looked intently at Peter for a moment and then said, "You are Simon, John's son—but you shall be called Peter, the rock!"

<sup>43</sup> The next day Jesus decided to go to Galilee. He found Philip and told him, "Come with me." <sup>44</sup> (Philip was from Bethsaida, Andrew and Peter's home town.)

<sup>45</sup> Philip now went off to look for Nathanael and told him, "We have found the Messiah!—the very person Moses and the prophets told about! His name is Jesus, the son of Joseph from Nazareth!"

<sup>46</sup> "Nazareth!" exclaimed Nathanael. "Can anything good come from there?"

"Just come and see for yourself," Philip declared.

<sup>47</sup> As they approached, Jesus said, "Here comes an honest man—a true son of Israel."

⁴⁸ "How do you know what I am like?" Nathanael demanded.

And Jesus replied, "I could see you under the fig tree before Philip found you."

⁴⁹ Nathanael replied, "Sir, you are the Son of God—the King of Israel!"

⁵⁰ Jesus asked him, "Do you believe all this just because I told you I had seen you under the fig tree? You will see greater proofs than this. ⁵¹ You will even see heaven open and the angels of God coming back and forth to me, the Messiah."

**2** Two days later Jesus' mother was a guest at a wedding in the village of Cana in Galilee, ² and Jesus and his disciples were invited too. ³ The wine supply ran out during the festivities, and Jesus' mother came to him with the problem.

⁴ "I can't help you now," he said. "It isn't yet my time for miracles."

⁵ But his mother told the servants, "Do whatever he tells you to."

⁶ Six stone waterpots were standing there; they were used for Jewish ceremonial purposes and held perhaps twenty to thirty gallons each. ⁷·⁸ Then Jesus told the servants to fill them to the brim with water. When this was done he said, "Dip some out and take it to the master of ceremonies."

⁹ When the master of ceremonies tasted the water that was now wine, not knowing where it had come from (though, of course, the servants did), he called the bridegroom over.

¹⁰ "This is wonderful stuff!" he said. "You're

different from most. Usually a host uses the best wine first, and afterwards, when everyone is full and doesn't care, then he brings out the less expensive brands. But you have kept the best for the last!"

<sup>11</sup> This miracle at Cana in Galilee was Jesus' first public demonstration of his heaven-sent power. And his disciples believed that he really was the Messiah.

<sup>12</sup> After the wedding he left for Capernaum for a few days with his mother, brothers, and disciples.

<sup>13</sup> Then it was time for the annual Jewish Passover celebration, and Jesus went to Jerusalem.

<sup>14</sup> In the Temple area he saw merchants selling cattle, sheep, and doves for sacrifices, and moneychangers behind their counters. <sup>15</sup> Jesus made a whip from some ropes and chased them all out, and drove out the sheep and oxen, scattering the moneychangers' coins over the floor and turning over their tables! <sup>16</sup> Then, going over to the men selling doves, he told them, "Get these things out of here. Don't turn my Father's House into a market!"

<sup>17</sup> Then his disciples remembered this prophecy from the Scriptures: "Concern for God's House will be my undoing."

<sup>18</sup> "What right have you to order them out?" the Jewish leaders demanded. "If you have this authority from God, show us a miracle to prove it."

<sup>19</sup> "All right," Jesus replied, "this is the miracle I will do for you: Destroy this sanctuary and in three days I will raise it up!"

<sup>20</sup> "What!" they exclaimed. "It took forty-six years to build this Temple, and you can do it in three days?" <sup>21</sup> But by "this sanctuary" he meant his body. <sup>22</sup> After he came back to life again, the disciples remembered his saying this and realized that what he had quoted from the Scriptures really did refer to him, and had all come true!

<sup>23</sup> Because of the miracles he did in Jerusalem at the Passover celebration, many people were convinced that he was indeed the Messiah. <sup>24, 25</sup> But Jesus didn't trust them, for he knew mankind to the core. No one needed to tell him how changeable human nature is!

**3** After dark one night a Jewish religious leader named Nicodemus, a member of the sect of the Pharisees, came for an interview with Jesus. "Sir," he said, "we all know that God has sent you to teach us. Your miracles are proof enough of this."

<sup>3</sup> Jesus replied, "With all the earnestness I possess I tell you this: Unless you are born again, you can never get into the Kingdom of God."

<sup>4</sup> "Born again!" exclaimed Nicodemus. "What do you mean? How can an old man go back into his mother's womb and be born again?"

<sup>5</sup> Jesus replied, "What I am telling you so earnestly is this: Unless one is born of water and the Spirit, he cannot enter the Kingdom of God. <sup>6</sup> Men can only reproduce human life, but the Holy Spirit gives new life from heaven; <sup>7</sup> so don't be surprised at my statement that you must be born again! <sup>8</sup> Just as you can hear the wind but can't tell where it comes from or where it will go

next, so it is with the Spirit. We do not know on whom he will next bestow this life from heaven."

9 "What do you mean?" Nicodemus asked.

10, 11 Jesus replied, "You, a respected Jewish teacher, and yet you don't understand these things? I am telling you what I know and have seen—and yet you won't believe me. 12 But if you don't even believe me when I tell you about such things as these that happen here among men, how can you possibly believe if I tell you what is going on in heaven? 13 For only I, the Messiah, have come to earth and will return to heaven again. 14 And as Moses in the wilderness lifted up the bronze image of a serpent on a pole, even so I must be lifted up upon a pole, 15 so that anyone who believes in me will have eternal life. 16 For God loved the world so much that he gave his only Son so that anyone who believes in him shall not perish but have eternal life. 17 God did not send his Son into the world to condemn it, but to save it.

18 "There is no eternal doom awaiting those who trust him to save them. But those who don't trust him have already been tried and condemned for not believing in the only Son of God. 19 Their sentence is based on this fact: that the Light from heaven came into the world, but they loved the darkness more than the Light, for their deeds were evil. 20 They hated the heavenly Light because they wanted to sin in the darkness. They stayed away from that Light for fear their sins would be exposed and they would be punished. 21 But those doing right come gladly to the Light to let everyone see that they are doing what God wants them to."

<sup>22</sup> Afterwards Jesus and his disciples left Jerusalem and stayed for a while in Judea and baptized there.

<sup>23, 24</sup> At this time John the Baptist was not yet in prison. He was baptizing at Aenon, near Salim, because there was plenty of water there. <sup>25</sup> One day someone began an argument with John's disciples, telling them that Jesus' baptism was best. <sup>26</sup> So they came to John and said, "Master, the man you met on the other side of the Jordan River—the one you said was the Messiah—he is baptizing too, and everybody is going over there instead of coming here to us."

<sup>27</sup> John replied, "God in heaven appoints each man's work. <sup>28</sup> My work is to prepare the way for that man so that everyone will go to him. You yourselves know how plainly I told you that I am not the Messiah. I am here to prepare the way for him—that is all. <sup>29</sup> The crowds will naturally go to the main attraction—the bride will go where the bridegroom is! A bridegroom's friends rejoice with him. I am the Bridegroom's friend, and I am filled with joy at his success. <sup>30</sup> He must become greater and greater, and I must become less and less.

<sup>31</sup> "He has come from heaven and is greater than anyone else. I am of the earth, and my understanding is limited to the things of earth. <sup>32</sup> He tells what he has seen and heard, but how few believe what he tells them! <sup>33, 34</sup> Those who believe him discover that God is a fountain of truth. For this one—sent by God—speaks God's words, for God's Spirit is upon him without measure or limit. <sup>35</sup> The Father loves this man because he is his Son, and God has given him

everything there is. ³⁶ And all who trust him—
God's Son—to save them have eternal life; those
who don't believe and obey him shall never see
heaven, but the wrath of God remains upon
them."

**4** When the Lord knew that the Pharisees
had heard about the greater crowds
coming to him than to John to be
baptized and to become his disciples—(though
Jesus himself didn't baptize them, but his
disciples did)— ³ he left Judea and returned to
the province of Galilee.

⁴ He had to go through Samaria on the way,
⁵, ⁶ and around noon as he approached the village
of Sychar, he came to Jacob's Well, located on
the parcel of ground Jacob gave to his son
Joseph. Jesus was tired from the long walk in the
hot sun and sat wearily beside the well.

⁷ Soon a Samaritan woman came to draw
water, and Jesus asked her for a drink. ⁸ He was
alone at the time as his disciples had gone into
the village to buy some food. ⁹ The woman was
surprised that a Jew would ask a "despised
Samaritan" for anything—usually they wouldn't
even speak to them!—and she remarked about
this to Jesus.

¹⁰ He replied, "If you only knew what a
wonderful gift God has for you, and who I am,
you would ask me for some *living* water!"

¹¹ "But you don't have a rope or a bucket," she
said, "and this is a very deep well! Where would
you get this living water? ¹² And besides, are you
greater than our ancestor Jacob? How can you

offer better water than this which he and his
sons and cattle enjoyed?"

¹³ Jesus replied that people soon became thirsty
again after drinking this water. ¹⁴ "But the water
I give them," he said, "becomes a perpetual
spring within them, watering them forever with
eternal life."

¹⁵ "Please, sir," the woman said, "give me some
of that water! Then I'll never be thirsty again
and won't have to make this long trip out here
every day."

¹⁶ "Go and get your husband," Jesus told her.

¹⁷, ¹⁸ "But I'm not married," the woman replied.

"All too true!" Jesus said. "For you have had
five husbands, and you aren't even married to the
man you're living with now."

¹⁹ "Sir," the woman said, "you must be a
prophet. ²⁰ But say, tell me, why is it that you
Jews insist that Jerusalem is the only place of
worship, while we Samaritans claim it is here [at
Mount Gerazim], where our ancestors
worshiped?"

²¹⁻²⁴ Jesus replied, "The time is coming, ma'am,
when we will no longer be concerned about
whether to worship the Father here or in
Jerusalem. For it's not *where* we worship that
counts, but *how* we worship—is our worship
spiritual and real? Do we have the Holy Spirit's
help? For God is Spirit, and we must have his
help to worship as we should. The Father wants
this kind of worship from us. But you Samaritans
know so little about him, worshiping blindly,
while we Jews know all about him, for salvation
comes to the world through the Jews."

²⁵ The woman said, "Well, at least I know that

the Messiah will come—the one they call
Christ—and when he does, he will explain
everything to us."

²⁶ Then Jesus told her, "I am the Messiah!"

²⁷ Just then his disciples arrived. They were
surprised to find him talking to a woman, but
none of them asked him why, or what they had
been discussing.

²⁸, ²⁹ Then the woman left her waterpot beside
the well and went back to the village and told
everyone, "Come and meet a man who told me
everything I ever did! Can this be the Messiah?"
³⁰ So the people came streaming from the village
to see him.

³¹ Meanwhile, the disciples were urging Jesus
to eat. ³² "No," he said, "I have some food you
don't know about."

³³ "Who brought it to him?" the disciples asked
each other.

³⁴ Then Jesus explained: "My nourishment
comes from doing the will of God who sent me,
and from finishing his work. ³⁵ Do you think the
work of harvesting will not begin until the
summer ends four months from now? Look
around you! Vast fields of human souls are
ripening all around us, and are ready now for
reaping. ³⁶ The reapers will be paid good wages
and will be gathering eternal souls into the
granaries of heaven! What joys await the sower
and the reaper, both together! ³⁷ For it is true
that one sows and someone else reaps. ³⁸ I sent
you to reap where you didn't sow; others did the
work, and you received the harvest."

³⁹ Many from the Samaritan village believed he
was the Messiah because of the woman's report:

"He told me everything I ever did!" 40, 41 When
they came out to see him at the well, they begged
him to stay at their village; and he did, for two
days, long enough for many of them to believe in
him after hearing him. 42 Then they said to the
woman, "Now we believe because we have heard
him ourselves, not just because of what you told
us. He is indeed the Savior of the world."

43, 44 At the end of the two days' stay he went
on into Galilee. Jesus used to say, "A prophet is
honored everywhere except in his own country!"
45 But the Galileans welcomed him with open
arms, for they had been in Jerusalem at the
Passover celebration and had seen some of his
miracles.

46, 47 In the course of his journey through
Galilee he arrived at the town of Cana, where he
had turned the water into wine. While he was
there, a man in the city of Capernaum, a
government official, whose son was very sick,
heard that Jesus had come from Judea and was
traveling in Galilee. This man went over to Cana,
found Jesus, and begged him to come to
Capernaum with him and heal his son, who was
now at death's door.

48 Jesus asked, "Won't any of you believe in me
unless I do more and more miracles?"

49 The official pled, "Sir, please come now
before my child dies."

50 Then Jesus told him, "Go back home. Your
son is healed!" And the man believed Jesus and
started home. 51 While he was on his way, some
of his servants met him with the news that all
was well—his son had recovered. 52 He asked
them when the lad had begun to feel better, and

they replied, "Yesterday afternoon at about one o'clock his fever suddenly disappeared!" [53] Then the father realized it was the same moment that Jesus had told him, "Your son is healed." And the officer and his entire household believed that Jesus was the Messiah.

[54] This was Jesus' second miracle in Galilee after coming from Judea.

**5** Afterwards Jesus returned to Jerusalem for one of the Jewish religious holidays. [2] Inside the city, near the Sheep Gate, was Bethesda Pool, with five covered platforms or porches surrounding it. [3] Crowds of sick folks—lame, blind, or with paralyzed limbs—lay on the platforms (waiting for a certain movement of the water, [4] for an angel of the Lord came from time to time and disturbed the water, and the first person to step down into it afterwards was healed).

[5] One of the men lying there had been sick for thirty-eight years. [6] When Jesus saw him and knew how long he had been ill, he asked him, "Would you like to get well?"

[7] "I can't," the sick man said, "for I have no one to help me into the pool at the movement of the water. While I am trying to get there, someone else always gets in ahead of me."

[8] Jesus told him, "Stand up, roll up your sleeping mat and go on home!"

[9] Instantly, the man was healed! He rolled up the mat and began walking!

But it was on the Sabbath when this miracle was done. [10] So the Jewish leaders objected. They said to the man who was cured, "You can't work on the Sabbath! It's illegal to carry that sleeping mat!"

¹¹ "The man who healed me told me to," was his reply.

¹² "Who said such a thing as that?" they demanded.

¹³ The man didn't know, and Jesus had disappeared into the crowd. ¹⁴ But afterwards Jesus found him in the Temple and told him, "Now you are well; don't sin as you did before, or something even worse may happen to you."

¹⁵ Then the man went to find the Jewish leaders and told them it was Jesus who had healed him.

¹⁶ So they began harassing Jesus as a Sabbath breaker.

¹⁷ But Jesus replied, "My Father constantly does good, and I'm following his example."

¹⁸ Then the Jewish leaders were all the more eager to kill him because in addition to disobeying their Sabbath laws, he had spoken of God as his Father, thereby making himself equal with God.

¹⁹ Jesus replied, "The Son can do nothing by himself. He does only what he sees the Father doing, and in the same way. ²⁰ For the Father loves the Son, and tells him everything he is doing; and the Son will do far more awesome miracles than this man's healing. ²¹ He will even raise from the dead anyone he wants to, just as the Father does. ²² And the Father leaves all judgment of sin to his Son, ²³ so that everyone will honor the Son, just as they honor the Father. But if you refuse to honor God's Son, whom he

sent to you, then you are certainly not honoring the Father.

24 "I say emphatically that anyone who listens to my message and believes in God who sent me has eternal life, and will never be damned for his sins, but has already passed out of death into life.

25 "And I solemnly declare that the time is coming, in fact, it is here, when the dead shall hear my voice—the voice of the Son of God—and those who listen shall live. 26 The Father has life in himself, and has granted his Son to have life in himself, 27 and to judge the sins of all mankind because he is the Son of Man. 28 Don't be so surprised! Indeed the time is coming when all the dead in their graves shall hear the voice of God's Son, 29 and shall rise again—those who have done good, to eternal life; and those who have continued in evil, to judgment.

30 "But I pass no judgment without consulting the Father. I judge as I am told. And my judgment is absolutely fair and just, for it is according to the will of God who sent me and is not merely my own.

31 "When I make claims about myself they aren't believed, 32, 33 but someone else, yes, John the Baptist, is making these claims for me too. You have gone out to listen to his preaching, and I can assure you that all he says about me is true! 34 But the truest witness I have is not from a man, though I have reminded you about John's witness so that you will believe in me and be saved. 35 John shone brightly for a while, and you benefited and rejoiced, 36 but I have a greater witness than John. I refer to the miracles I do;

these have been assigned me by the Father, and they prove that the Father has sent me. [37] And the Father himself has also testified about me, though not appearing to you personally, or speaking to you directly. [38] But you are not listening to him, for you refuse to believe me—the one sent to you with God's message.

[39] "You search the Scriptures, for you believe they give you eternal life. And the Scriptures point to me! [40] Yet you won't come to me so that I can give you this life eternal!

[41, 42] "Your approval or disapproval means nothing to me, for as I know so well, you don't have God's love within you. [43] I know, because I have come to you representing my Father and you refuse to welcome me, though you readily enough receive those who aren't sent from him, but represent only themselves! [44] No wonder you can't believe! For you gladly honor each other, but you don't care about the honor that comes from the only God!

[45] "Yet it is not I who will accuse you of this to the Father—Moses will! Moses, on whose laws you set your hopes of heaven. [46] For you have refused to believe Moses. He wrote about me, but you refuse to believe him, so you refuse to believe in me. [47] And since you don't believe what he wrote, no wonder you don't believe me either."

**6** After this, Jesus crossed over the Sea of Galilee, also known as the Sea of Tiberias. [2-5] And a huge crowd, many of them pilgrims on their way to Jerusalem for the annual Passover celebration, were following him wherever he went, to watch him heal the sick. So when Jesus went up into the hills and sat down with his disciples around him, he soon saw a great multitude of people climbing the hill, looking for him.

Turning to Philip he asked, "Philip, where can we buy bread to feed all these people?" ⁶ (He was testing Philip, for he already knew what he was going to do.)

⁷ Philip replied, "It would take a fortune to begin to do it!"

⁸, ⁹ Then Andrew, Simon Peter's brother, spoke up. "There's a youngster here with five barley loaves and a couple of fish! But what good is that with all this mob?"

¹⁰ "Tell everyone to sit down," Jesus ordered. And all of them—the approximate count of the men only was 5,000—sat down on the grassy slopes. ¹¹ Then Jesus took the loaves and gave thanks to God and passed them out to the people. Afterwards he did the same with the fish. And everyone ate until full!

¹² "Now gather the scraps," Jesus told his disciples, "so that nothing is wasted." ¹³ And twelve baskets were filled with the leftovers!

¹⁴ When the people realized what a great miracle had happened, they exclaimed, "Surely, he is the Prophet we have been expecting!"

¹⁵ Jesus saw that they were ready to take him by force and make him their king, so he went higher into the mountains alone.

¹⁶ That evening his disciples went down to the shore to wait for him. ¹⁷ But as darkness fell and Jesus still hadn't come back, they got into the

boat and headed out across the lake toward
Capernaum. [18, 19] But soon a gale swept down
upon them as they rowed, and the sea grew very
rough. They were three or four miles out when
suddenly they saw Jesus walking toward the
boat! They were terrified, [20] but he called out to
them and told them not to be afraid. [21] Then they
were willing to let him in, and immediately the
boat was where they were going!

[22, 23] The next morning, back across the lake,
crowds began gathering on the shore [waiting to
see Jesus]. For they knew that he and his
disciples had come over together and that the
disciples had gone off in their boat, leaving him
behind. Several small boats from Tiberias were
nearby, [24] so when the people saw that Jesus
wasn't there, nor his disciples, they got into the
boats and went across to Capernaum to look for
him.

[25] When they arrived and found him, they said,
"Sir, how did you get here?" [26] Jesus replied,
"The truth of the matter is that you want to be
with me because I fed you, not because you
believe in me. [27] But you shouldn't be so
concerned about perishable things like food. No,
spend your energy seeking the eternal life that I,
the Messiah, can give you. For God the Father
has sent me for this very purpose."

[28] They replied, "What should we do to satisfy
God?"

[29] Jesus told them, "This is the will of God,
that you believe in the one he has sent."

[30, 31] They replied, "You must show us more
miracles if you want us to believe you are the
Messiah. Give us free bread every day, like our

fathers had while they journeyed through the wilderness! As the Scriptures say, 'Moses gave them bread from heaven.' "

32 Jesus said, "Moses didn't give it to them. My Father did. And now he offers you true Bread from heaven. 33 The true Bread is a Person—the one sent by God from heaven, and he gives life to the world."

34 "Sir," they said, "give us that bread every day of our lives!"

35 Jesus replied, "I am the Bread of Life. No one coming to me will ever be hungry again. Those believing in me will never thirst. 36 But the trouble is, as I have told you before, you haven't believed even though you have seen me. 37 But some will come to me—those the Father has given me—and I will never, never reject them. 38 For I have come here from heaven to do the will of God who sent me, not to have my own way. 39 And this is the will of God, that I should not lose even one of all those he has given me, but that I should raise them to eternal life at the Last Day. 40 For it is my Father's will that everyone who sees his Son and believes on him should have eternal life—that I should raise him at the Last Day."

41 Then the Jews began to murmur against him because he claimed to be the Bread from heaven.

42 "What?" they exclaimed. "Why, he is merely Jesus the son of Joseph, whose father and mother we know. What is this he is saying, that he came down from heaven?"

43 But Jesus replied, "Don't murmur among yourselves about my saying that. 44 For no one can come to me unless the Father who sent me

draws him to me, and at the Last Day I will cause all such to rise again from the dead. 45 As it is written in the Scriptures, 'They shall all be taught of God.' Those the Father speaks to, who learn the truth from him, will be attracted to me. 46 (Not that anyone actually sees the Father, for only I have seen him.)

47 "How earnestly I tell you this—anyone who believes in me already has eternal life! 48-51 Yes, I am the Bread of Life! When your fathers in the wilderness ate bread from the skies, they all died. But the Bread from heaven gives eternal life to everyone who eats it. I am that Living Bread that came down out of heaven. Anyone eating this Bread shall live forever; this Bread is my flesh given to redeem humanity."

52 Then the Jews began arguing with each other about what he meant. "How can this man give us his flesh to eat?" they asked.

53 So Jesus said it again, "With all the earnestness I possess I tell you this: Unless you eat the flesh of the Messiah and drink his blood, you cannot have eternal life within you. 54 But anyone who does eat my flesh and drink my blood has eternal life, and I will raise him at the Last Day. 55 For my flesh is the true food, and my blood is the true drink. 56 Everyone who eats my flesh and drinks my blood is in me, and I in him. 57 I live by the power of the living Father who sent me, and in the same way those who partake of me shall live because of me! 58 I am the true Bread from heaven; and anyone who eats this Bread shall live forever, and not die as your fathers did—though they ate bread from

heaven." ⁵⁹ (He preached this sermon in the synagogue in Capernaum.)

⁶⁰ Even his disciples said, "This is very hard to understand. Who can tell what he means?"

⁶¹ Jesus knew within himself that his disciples were complaining and said to them, "Does *this* offend you? ⁶² Then what will you think if you see me, the Messiah, return to heaven again? ⁶³ Only the Holy Spirit gives eternal life. Those born only once, with physical birth, will never receive this gift. But now I have told you how to get this true spiritual life. ⁶⁴ But some of you don't believe me." (For Jesus knew from the beginning who didn't believe and knew the one who would betray him.)

⁶⁵ And he remarked, "That is what I meant when I said that no one can come to me unless the Father attracts him to me."

⁶⁶ At this point many of his disciples turned away and deserted him.

⁶⁷ Then Jesus turned to the Twelve and asked, "Are you going too?"

⁶⁸ Simon Peter replied, "Master, to whom shall we go? You alone have the words that give eternal life, ⁶⁹ and we believe them and know you are the holy Son of God."

⁷⁰ Then Jesus said, "I chose the twelve of you, and one is a devil." ⁷¹ He was speaking of Judas, son of Simon Iscariot, one of the Twelve, who would betray him.

**7** After this, Jesus went to Galilee, going from village to village, for he wanted to stay out of Judea where the Jewish leaders were plotting his death. ² But soon it was time for the Tabernacle Ceremonies, one of the annual Jewish holidays, ³ and Jesus' brothers urged him to go to Judea for the celebration.

"Go where more people can see your miracles!" they scoffed. ⁴ "You can't be famous when you hide like this! If you're so great, prove it to the world!" ⁵ For even his brothers didn't believe in him.

⁶ Jesus replied, "It is not the right time for me to go now. But you can go anytime and it will make no difference, ⁷ for the world can't hate you; but it does hate me, because I accuse it of sin and evil. ⁸ You go on, and I'll come later when it is the right time." ⁹ So he remained in Galilee.

¹⁰ But after his brothers had left for the celebration, then he went too, though secretly, staying out of the public eye. ¹¹ The Jewish leaders tried to find him at the celebration and kept asking if anyone had seen him. ¹² There was a lot of discussion about him among the crowds. Some said, "He's a wonderful man," while others said, "No, he's duping the public." ¹³ But no one had the courage to speak out for him in public for fear of reprisals from the Jewish leaders.

¹⁴ Then, midway through the festival, Jesus went up to the Temple and preached openly. ¹⁵ The Jewish leaders were surprised when they heard him. "How can he know so much when he's never been to our schools?" they asked.

¹⁶ So Jesus told them, "I'm not teaching you my own thoughts, but those of God who sent me. ¹⁷ If any of you really determines to do God's will, then you will certainly know whether my

teaching is from God or is merely my own.
¹⁸ Anyone presenting his own ideas is looking for
praise for himself, but anyone seeking to honor
the one who sent him is a good and true person.
¹⁹ None of *you* obeys the laws of Moses! So why
pick on *me* for breaking them? Why kill *me* for
this?"

²⁰ The crowd replied, "You're out of your mind!
Who's trying to kill you?"

²¹, ²², ²³ Jesus replied, "I worked on the Sabbath
by healing a man, and you were surprised. But
you work on the Sabbath, too, whenever you
obey Moses' law of circumcision (actually,
however, this tradition of circumcision is older
than the Mosaic law); for if the correct time for
circumcising your children falls on the Sabbath,
you go ahead and do it, as you should. So why
should I be condemned for making a man
completely well on the Sabbath? ²⁴ Think this
through and you will see that I am right."

²⁵ Some of the people who lived there in
Jerusalem said among themselves, "Isn't this the
man they are trying to kill? ²⁶ But here he is
preaching in public, and they say nothing to him.
Can it be that our leaders have learned, after all,
that he really is the Messiah? ²⁷ But how could
he be? For we know where this man was born;
when Christ comes, he will just appear and no
one will know where he comes from."

²⁸ So Jesus, in a sermon in the Temple, called
out, "Yes, you know me and where I was born
and raised, but I am the representative of one
you don't know, and he is Truth. ²⁹ I know him
because I was with him, and he sent me to you."

³⁰ Then the Jewish leaders sought to arrest

him; but no hand was laid on him, for God's time had not yet come.

31 Many among the crowds at the Temple believed on him. "After all," they said, "what miracles do you expect the Messiah to do that this man hasn't done?"

32 When the Pharisees heard that the crowds were in this mood, they and the chief priests sent officers to arrest Jesus. 33 But Jesus told them, "[Not yet!] I am to be here a little longer. Then I shall return to the one who sent me. 34 You will search for me but not find me. And you won't be able to come where I am!"

35 The Jewish leaders were puzzled by this statement. "Where is he planning to go?" they asked. "Maybe he is thinking of leaving the country and going as a missionary among the Jews in other lands, or maybe even to the Gentiles! 36 What does he mean about our looking for him and not being able to find him, and, 'You won't be able to come where I am'?"

37 On the last day, the climax of the holidays, Jesus shouted to the crowds, "If anyone is thirsty, let him come to me and drink. 38 For the Scriptures declare that rivers of living water shall flow from the inmost being of anyone who believes in me." 39 (He was speaking of the Holy Spirit, who would be given to everyone believing in him; but the Spirit had not yet been given, because Jesus had not yet returned to his glory in heaven.)

40 When the crowds heard him say this, some of them declared, "This man surely is the prophet who will come just before the Messiah."

41, 42 Others said, "He *is* the Messiah." Still others,

"But he *can't* be! Will the Messiah come from *Galilee?* For the Scriptures clearly state that the Messiah will be born of the royal line of David, in *Bethlehem*, the village where David was born."
43 So the crowd was divided about him. 44 And some wanted him arrested, but no one touched him.

45 The Temple police who had been sent to arrest him returned to the chief priests and Pharisees. "Why didn't you bring him in?" they demanded.

46 "He says such wonderful things!" they mumbled. "We've never heard anything like it."

47 "So you also have been led astray?" the Pharisees mocked. 48 "Is there a single one of us Jewish rulers or Pharisees who believes he is the Messiah? 49 These stupid crowds do, yes; but what do they know about it? A curse upon them anyway!"

50 Then Nicodemus spoke up. (Remember him? He was the Jewish leader who came secretly to interview Jesus.) 51 "Is it legal to convict a man before he is even tried?" he asked.

52 They replied, "Are you a wretched Galilean too? Search the Scriptures and see for yourself—no prophets will come from Galilee!"

53 Then the meeting broke up and everybody went home.

**8** Jesus returned to the Mount of Olives, 2 but early the next morning he was back again at the Temple. A crowd soon gathered, and he sat down and talked to them. 3 As he was speaking, the Jewish leaders and

Pharisees brought a woman caught in adultery and placed her out in front of the staring crowd.

⁴ "Teacher," they said to Jesus, "this woman was caught in the very act of adultery. ⁵ Moses' law says to kill her. What about it?"

⁶ They were trying to trap him into saying something they could use against him, but Jesus stooped down and wrote in the dust with his finger. ⁷ They kept demanding an answer, so he stood up again and said, "All right, hurl the stones at her until she dies. But only he who never sinned may throw the first!"

⁸ Then he stooped down again and wrote some more in the dust. ⁹ And the Jewish leaders slipped away one by one, beginning with the eldest, until only Jesus was left in front of the crowd with the woman.

¹⁰ Then Jesus stood up again and said to her, "Where are your accusers? Didn't even one of them condemn you?"

¹¹ "No, sir," she said.

And Jesus said, "Neither do I. Go and sin no more."

¹² Later, in one of his talks, Jesus said to the people, "I am the Light of the world. So if you follow me, you won't be stumbling through the darkness, for living light will flood your path."

¹³ The Pharisees replied, "You are boasting—and lying!"

¹⁴ Jesus told them, "These claims are true even though I make them concerning myself. For I know where I came from and where I am going, but you don't know this about me. ¹⁵ You pass judgment on me without knowing the facts. I am not judging you now; ¹⁶ but if I were, it would be

an absolutely correct judgment in every respect, for I have with me the Father who sent me. [17] Your laws say that if two men agree on something that has happened, their witness is accepted as fact. [18] Well, I am one witness, and my Father who sent me is the other.''

[19] "Where is your father?'' they asked.

Jesus answered, "You don't know who I am, so you don't know who my Father is. If you knew me, then you would know him too.''

[20] Jesus made these statements while in the section of the Temple known as the Treasury. But he was not arrested, for his time had not yet run out.

[21] Later he said to them again, "I am going away; and you will search for me, and die in your sins. And you cannot come where I am going.''

[22] The Jews asked, "Is he planning suicide? What does he mean, 'You cannot come where I am going'?''

[23] Then he said to them, "You are from below; I am from above. You are of this world; I am not. [24] That is why I said that you will die in your sins; for unless you believe that I am the Messiah, the Son of God, you will die in your sins.''

[25] "Tell us who you are,'' they demanded.

He replied, "I am the one I have always claimed to be. [26] I could condemn you for much and teach you much, but I won't, for I say only what I am told to by the one who sent me; and he is Truth.'' [27] But they still didn't understand that he was talking to them about God.

[28] So Jesus said, "When you have killed the

Messiah, then you will realize that I am he and that I have not been telling you my own ideas, but have spoken what the Father taught me. ²⁹ And he who sent me is with me—he has not deserted me—for I always do those things that are pleasing to him."

³⁰,³¹ Then many of the Jewish leaders who heard him say these things began believing him to be the Messiah.

Jesus said to them, "You are truly my disciples if you live as I tell you to, ³² and you will know the truth, and the truth will set you free."

³³ "But we are descendants of Abraham," they said, "and have never been slaves to any man on earth! What do you mean, 'set free'?"

³⁴ Jesus replied, "You are slaves of sin, every one of you. ³⁵ And slaves don't have rights, but the Son has every right there is! ³⁶ So if the Son sets you free, you will indeed be free— ³⁷ (Yes, I realize that you are descendants of Abraham!) And yet some of you are trying to kill me because my message does not find a home within your hearts. ³⁸ I am telling you what I saw when I was with my Father. But you are following the advice of *your* father."

³⁹ "Our father is Abraham," they declared.

"No!" Jesus replied, "for if he were, you would follow his good example. ⁴⁰ But instead you are trying to kill me—and all because I told you the truth I heard from God. Abraham wouldn't do a thing like that! ⁴¹ No, you are obeying your *real* father when you act that way."

They replied, "We were not born out of wedlock—our true Father is God himself."

⁴² Jesus told them, "If that were so, then you

would love me, for I have come to you from God. I am not here on my own, but he sent me. ⁴³ Why can't you understand what I am saying? It is because you are prevented from doing so! ⁴⁴ For you are the children of your father the devil and you love to do the evil things he does. He was a murderer from the beginning and a hater of truth—there is not an iota of truth in him. When he lies, it is perfectly normal; for he is the father of liars. ⁴⁵ And so when I tell the truth, you just naturally don't believe it!

⁴⁶ "Which of you can truthfully accuse me of one single sin? [No one!] And since I am telling you the truth, why don't you believe me? ⁴⁷ Anyone whose Father is God listens gladly to the words of God. Since you don't, it proves you aren't his children."

⁴⁸ "You Samaritan! Foreigner! Devil!" the Jewish leaders snarled. "Didn't we say all along you were possessed by a demon?"

⁴⁹ "No," Jesus said, "I have no demon in me. For I honor my Father—and you dishonor me. ⁵⁰ And though I have no wish to make myself great, God wants this for me and judges [those who reject me]. ⁵¹ With all the earnestness I have I tell you this—no one who obeys me shall ever die!"

⁵² The leaders of the Jews said, "Now we know you are possessed by a demon. Even Abraham and the mightiest prophets died, and yet you say that obeying you will keep a man from dying! ⁵³ So you are greater than our father Abraham, who died? And greater than the prophets, who died? Who do you think you are?" ⁵⁴ Then Jesus told them this: "If I am merely boasting about

myself, it doesn't count. But it is my Father—and you claim him as your God—who is saying these glorious things about me. [55] But you do not even know him. I do. If I said otherwise, I would be as great a liar as you! But it is true—I know him and fully obey him. [56] Your father Abraham rejoiced to see my day. He knew I was coming and was glad."

[57] *The Jewish leaders:* "You aren't even fifty years old—sure, you've seen Abraham!"

[58] *Jesus:* "The absolute truth is that I was in existence before Abraham was ever born!"

[59] At that point the Jewish leaders picked up stones to kill him. But Jesus was hidden from them, and walked past them and left the Temple.

**9** As he was walking along, he saw a man blind from birth.

[2] "Master," his disciples asked him, "why was this man born blind? Was it a result of his own sins or those of his parents?"

[3] "Neither," Jesus answered. "But to demonstrate the power of God. [4] All of us must quickly carry out the tasks assigned us by the one who sent me, for there is little time left before the night falls and all work comes to an end. [5] But while I am still here in the world, I give it my light."

[6] Then he spat on the ground and made mud from the spittle and smoothed the mud over the blind man's eyes, [7] and told him, "Go and wash in the Pool of Siloam" (the word "Siloam" means "Sent"). So the man went where he was sent and washed and came back seeing!

[8] His neighbors and others who knew him as a blind beggar asked each other, "Is this the same fellow—that beggar?"

[9] Some said yes, and some said no. "It can't be the same man," they thought, "but he surely looks like him!"

And the beggar said, "I *am* the same man!"

[10] Then they asked him how in the world he could see. What had happened?

[11] And he told them, "A man they call Jesus made mud and smoothed it over my eyes and told me to go to the Pool of Siloam and wash off the mud. I did, and I can see!"

[12] "Where is he now?" they asked.

"I don't know," he replied.

[13] Then they took the man to the Pharisees. [14] Now as it happened, this all occurred on a Sabbath. [15] Then the Pharisees asked him all about it. So he told them how Jesus had smoothed the mud over his eyes, and when it was washed away, he could see!

[16] Some of them said, "Then this fellow Jesus is not from God, because he is working on the Sabbath."

Others said, "But how could an ordinary sinner do such miracles?" So there was a deep division of opinion among them.

[17] Then the Pharisees turned on the man who had been blind and demanded, "This man who opened your eyes—who do you say he is?"

"I think he must be a prophet sent from God," the man replied.

[18] The Jewish leaders wouldn't believe he had been blind, until they called in his parents [19] and

asked them, "Is this your son? Was he born blind? If so, how can he see?"

²⁰ His parents replied, "We know this is our son and that he was born blind, ²¹ but we don't know what happened to make him see, or who did it. He is old enough to speak for himself. Ask him."

²²,²³ They said this in fear of the Jewish leaders who had announced that anyone saying Jesus was the Messiah would be excommunicated.

²⁴ So for the second time they called in the man who had been blind and told him, "Give the glory to God, not to Jesus, for we know Jesus is an evil person."

²⁵ "I don't know whether he is good or bad," the man replied, "but I know this: *I was blind, and now I see!*"

²⁶ "But what did he do?" they asked. "How did he heal you?"

²⁷ "Look!" the man exclaimed. "I told you once; didn't you listen? Why do you want to hear it again? Do you want to become his disciples too?"

²⁸ Then they cursed him and said, "You are his disciple, but we are disciples of Moses. ²⁹ We know God has spoken to Moses, but as for this fellow, we don't know anything about him."

³⁰ "Why, that's very strange!" the man replied. "He can heal blind men, and yet you don't know anything about him! ³¹ Well, God doesn't listen to evil men, but he has open ears to those who worship him and do his will. ³² Since the world began there has never been anyone who could open the eyes of someone born blind. ³³ If this man were not from God, he couldn't do it."

³⁴ "You illegitimate bastard, you!" they shouted. "Are you trying to teach *us?*" And they threw him out.

³⁵ When Jesus heard what had happened, he found the man and said, "Do you believe in the Messiah?"

³⁶ The man answered, "Who is he, sir, for I want to."

³⁷ "You have seen him," Jesus said, "and he is speaking to you!"

³⁸ "Yes, Lord," the man said, "I believe!" And he worshiped Jesus.

³⁹ Then Jesus told him, "I have come into the world to give sight to those who are spiritually blind and to show those who think they see that they are blind."

⁴⁰ The Pharisees who were standing there asked, "Are you saying we are blind?"

⁴¹ "If you were blind, you wouldn't be guilty," Jesus replied. "But your guilt remains because you claim to know what you are doing.

**10** "Anyone refusing to walk through the gate into a sheepfold, who sneaks over the wall, must surely be a thief! ² For a shepherd comes through the gate. ³ The gatekeeper opens the gate for him, and the sheep hear his voice and come to him; and he calls his own sheep by name and leads them out. ⁴ He walks ahead of them; and they follow him, for they recognize his voice. ⁵ They won't follow a stranger but will run from him, for they don't recognize his voice."

⁶ Those who heard Jesus use this illustration

didn't understand what he meant, [7] so he explained it to them.

"I am the Gate for the sheep," he said. [8] "All others who came before me were thieves and robbers. But the true sheep did not listen to them. [9] Yes, I am the Gate. Those who come in by way of the Gate will be saved and will go in and out and find green pastures. [10] The thief's purpose is to steal, kill and destroy. My purpose is to give life in all its fullness.

[11] "I am the Good Shepherd. The Good Shepherd lays down his life for the sheep. [12] A hired man will run when he sees a wolf coming and will leave the sheep, for they aren't his and he isn't their shepherd. And so the wolf leaps on them and scatters the flock. [13] The hired man runs because he is hired and has no real concern for the sheep.

[14] "I am the Good Shepherd and know my own sheep, and they know me, [15] just as my Father knows me and I know the Father; and I lay down my life for the sheep. [16] I have other sheep, too, in another fold. I must bring them also, and they will heed my voice; and there will be one flock with one Shepherd.

[17] "The Father loves me because I lay down my life that I may have it back again. [18] No one can kill me without my consent—I lay down my life voluntarily. For I have the right and power to lay it down when I want to and also the right and power to take it again. For the Father has given me this right."

[19] When he said these things, the Jewish leaders were again divided in their opinions

about him. [20] Some of them said, "He has a demon or else is crazy. Why listen to a man like that?"

[21] Others said, "This doesn't sound to us like a man possessed by a demon! Can a demon open the eyes of blind men?"

[22, 23] It was winter, and Jesus was in Jerusalem at the time of the Dedication Celebration. He was at the Temple, walking through the section known as Solomon's Hall. [24] The Jewish leaders surrounded him and asked, "How long are you going to keep us in suspense? If you are the Messiah, tell us plainly."

[25] "I have already told you, and you don't believe me," Jesus replied. "The proof is in the miracles I do in the name of my Father. [26] But you don't believe me because you are not part of my flock. [27] My sheep recognize my voice, and I know them, and they follow me. [28] I give them eternal life and they shall never perish. No one shall snatch them away from me, [29] for my Father has given them to me, and he is more powerful than anyone else, so no one can kidnap them from me. [30] I and the Father are one."

[31] Then again the Jewish leaders picked up stones to kill him.

[32] Jesus said, "At God's direction I have done many a miracle to help the people. For which one are you killing me?"

[33] They replied, "Not for any good work, but for blasphemy; you, a mere man, have declared yourself to be God."

[34, 35, 36] "In your own Law it says that men are gods!" he replied. "So if the Scripture, which cannot be untrue, speaks of those as gods to whom the message of God came, do you call it blasphemy when the one sanctified and sent into the world by the Father says, 'I am the Son of God'? ³⁷ Don't believe me unless I do miracles of God. ³⁸ But if I do, believe them even if you don't believe me. Then you will become convinced that the Father is in me, and I in the Father."

³⁹ Once again they started to arrest him. But he walked away and left them, ⁴⁰ and went beyond the Jordan River to stay near the place where John was first baptizing. ⁴¹ And many followed him.

"John didn't do miracles," they remarked to one another, "but all his predictions concerning this man have come true." ⁴² And many came to the decision that he was the Messiah.

**11** Do you remember Mary, who poured the costly perfume on Jesus' feet and wiped them with her hair? Well, her brother Lazarus, who lived in Bethany with Mary and her sister Martha, was sick. ³ So the two sisters sent a message to Jesus telling him, "Sir, your good friend is very, very sick."

⁴ But when Jesus heard about it he said, "The purpose of his illness is not death, but for the glory of God. I, the Son of God, will receive glory from this situation."

⁵ Although Jesus was very fond of Martha, Mary, and Lazarus, ⁶ he stayed where he was for the next two days and made no move to go to them. ⁷ Finally, after the two days, he said to his disciples, "Let's go to Judea."

⁸ But his disciples objected. "Master," they

said, "only a few days ago the Jewish leaders in Judea were trying to kill you. Are you going there again?"

⁹ Jesus replied, "There are twelve hours of daylight every day, and during every hour of it a man can walk safely and not stumble. ¹⁰ Only at night is there danger of a wrong step, because of the dark." ¹¹ Then he said, "Our friend Lazarus has gone to sleep, but now I will go and waken him!"

¹², ¹³ The disciples, thinking Jesus meant Lazarus was having a good night's rest, said, "That means he is getting better!" But Jesus meant Lazarus had died.

¹⁴ Then he told them plainly, "Lazarus is dead. ¹⁵ And for your sake, I am glad I wasn't there, for this will give you another opportunity to believe in me. Come, let's go to him."

¹⁶ Thomas, nicknamed "The Twin," said to his fellow disciples, "Let's go too—and die with him."

¹⁷ When they arrived at Bethany, they were told that Lazarus had already been in his tomb for four days. ¹⁸ Bethany was only a couple of miles down the road from Jerusalem, ¹⁹ and many of the Jewish leaders had come to pay their respects and to console Martha and Mary on their loss. ²⁰ When Martha got word that Jesus was coming, she went to meet him. But Mary stayed at home.

²¹ Martha said to Jesus, "Sir, if you had been here, my brother wouldn't have died. ²² And even now it's not too late, for I know that God will bring my brother back to life again, if you will only ask him to."

²³ Jesus told her, "Your brother will come back to life again."

²⁴ "Yes," Martha said, "when everyone else does, on Resurrection Day."

²⁵ Jesus told her, "I am the one who raises the dead and gives them life again. Anyone who believes in me, even though he dies like anyone else, shall live again. ²⁶ He is given eternal life for believing in me and shall never perish. Do you believe this, Martha?"

²⁷ "Yes, Master," she told him. "I believe you are the Messiah, the Son of God, the one we have so long awaited."

²⁸ Then she left him and returned to Mary and, calling her aside from the mourners, told her, "He is here and wants to see you." ²⁹ So Mary went to him at once.

³⁰ Now Jesus had stayed outside the village, at the place where Martha met him. ³¹ When the Jewish leaders who were at the house trying to console Mary saw her leave so hastily, they assumed she was going to Lazarus' tomb to weep; so they followed her.

³² When Mary arrived where Jesus was, she fell down at his feet, saying, "Sir, if you had been here, my brother would still be alive."

³³ When Jesus saw her weeping and the Jewish leaders wailing with her, he was moved with indignation and deeply troubled. ³⁴ "Where is he buried?" he asked them.

They told him, "Come and see." ³⁵ Tears came to Jesus' eyes.

³⁶ "They were close friends," the Jewish leaders said. "See how much he loved him."

37, 38 But some said, "This fellow healed a blind man—why couldn't he keep Lazarus from dying?"

And again Jesus was moved with deep anger. Then they came to the tomb. It was a cave with a heavy stone rolled across its door.

39 "Roll the stone aside," Jesus told them.

But Martha, the dead man's sister, said, "By now the smell will be terrible, for he has been dead four days."

40 "But didn't I tell you that you will see a wonderful miracle from God if you believe?" Jesus asked her.

41 So they rolled the stone aside. Then Jesus looked up to heaven and said, "Father, thank you for hearing me. 42 (You always hear me, of course, but I said it because of all these people standing here, so that they will believe you sent me.)" 43 Then he shouted, "Lazarus, come out!"

44 And Lazarus came—bound up in the gravecloth, his face muffled in a head swath. Jesus told them, "Unwrap him and let him go!"

45 And so at last many of the Jewish leaders who were with Mary and saw it happen, finally believed on him. 46 But some went away to the Pharisees and reported it to them.

47 Then the chief priests and Pharisees convened a council to discuss the situation.

"What are we going to do?" they asked each other. "For this man certainly does miracles. 48 If we let him alone the whole nation will follow him—and then the Roman army will come and kill us and take over the Jewish government."

49 And one of them, Caiaphas, who was High Priest that year, said, "You stupid idiots— 50 let

this one man die for the people—why should the whole nation perish?"

⁵¹ This prophecy that Jesus should die for the entire nation came from Caiaphas in his position as High Priest—he didn't think of it by himself, but was inspired to say it. ⁵² It was a prediction that Jesus' death would not be for Israel only, but for all the children of God scattered around the world. ⁵³ So from that time on the Jewish leaders began plotting Jesus' death.

⁵⁴ Jesus now stopped his public ministry and left Jerusalem; he went to the edge of the desert, to the village of Ephraim, and stayed there with his disciples.

⁵⁵ The Passover, a Jewish holy day, was near, and many country people arrived in Jerusalem several days early so that they could go through the cleansing ceremony before the Passover began. ⁵⁶ They wanted to see Jesus, and as they gossiped in the Temple, they asked each other, "What do you think? Will he come for the Passover?" ⁵⁷ Meanwhile the chief priests and Pharisees had publicly announced that anyone seeing Jesus must report him immediately so that they could arrest him.

**12** Six days before the Passover ceremonies began, Jesus arrived in Bethany where Lazarus was—the man he had brought back to life. ² A banquet was prepared in Jesus' honor. Martha served, and Lazarus sat at the table with him. ³ Then Mary took a jar of costly perfume made from essence of nard, and anointed Jesus' feet with it and wiped them with her hair. And the house was filled with fragrance.

⁴ But Judas Iscariot, one of his disciples—the one who would betray him—said, ⁵ "That perfume was worth a fortune. It should have been sold and the money given to the poor." ⁶ Not that he cared for the poor, but he was in charge of the disciples' funds and often dipped into them for his own use!

⁷ Jesus replied, "Let her alone. She did it in preparation for my burial. ⁸ You can always help the poor, but I won't be with you very long."

⁹ When the ordinary people of Jerusalem heard of his arrival, they flocked to see him and also to see Lazarus—the man who had come back to life again. ¹⁰ Then the chief priests decided to kill Lazarus too, ¹¹ for it was because of him that many of the Jewish leaders had deserted and believed in Jesus as their Messiah.

¹² The next day, the news that Jesus was on the way to Jerusalem swept through the city, and a huge crowd of Passover visitors ¹³ took palm branches and went down the road to meet him, shouting, "The Savior! God bless the King of Israel! Hail to God's Ambassador!"

¹⁴ Jesus rode along on a young donkey, fulfilling the prophecy that said: ¹⁵ "Don't be afraid of your King, people of Israel, for he will come to you meekly, sitting on a donkey's colt!"

¹⁶ (His disciples didn't realize at the time that this was a fulfillment of prophecy; but after Jesus returned to his glory in heaven, then they noticed how many prophecies of Scripture had come true before their eyes.)

¹⁷ And those in the crowd who had seen Jesus

call Lazarus back to life were telling all about it. [18] That was the main reason why so many went out to meet him—because they had heard about this mighty miracle.

[19] Then the Pharisees said to each other, "We've lost. Look—the whole world has gone after him!"

[20] Some Greeks who had come to Jerusalem to attend the Passover [21] paid a visit to Philip, who was from Bethsaida, and said, "Sir, we want to meet Jesus." [22] Philip told Andrew about it, and they went together to ask Jesus.

[23, 24] Jesus replied that the time had come for him to return to his glory in heaven, and that "I must fall and die like a kernel of wheat that falls into the furrows of the earth. Unless I die I will be alone—a single seed. But my death will produce many new wheat kernels—a plentiful harvest of new lives. [25] If you love your life down here—you will lose it. If you despise your life down here—you will exchange it for eternal glory.

[26] "If these Greeks want to be my disciples, tell them to come and follow me, for my servants must be where I am. And if they follow me, the Father will honor them. [27] Now my soul is deeply troubled. Shall I pray, 'Father, save me from what lies ahead'? But that is the very reason why I came! [28] Father, bring glory and honor to your name."

Then a voice spoke from heaven saying, "I have already done this, and I will do it again." [29] When the crowd heard the voice, some of them thought it was thunder, while others declared an angel had spoken to him.

<sup>30</sup> Then Jesus told them, "The voice was for your benefit, not mine. <sup>31</sup> The time of judgment for the world has come—and the time when Satan, the prince of this world, shall be cast out. <sup>32</sup> And when I am lifted up [on the cross], I will draw everyone to me." <sup>33</sup> He said this to indicate how he was going to die.

<sup>34</sup> "Die?" asked the crowd. "We understood that the Messiah would live forever and never die. Why are you saying he will die? What Messiah are you talking about?"

<sup>35</sup> Jesus replied, "My light will shine out for you just a little while longer. Walk in it while you can, and go where you want to go before the darkness falls, for then it will be too late for you to find your way. <sup>36</sup> Make use of the Light while there is still time; then you will become light bearers."

After saying these things, Jesus went away and was hidden from them.

<sup>37</sup> But despite all the miracles he had done, most of the people would not believe he was the Messiah. <sup>38</sup> This is exactly what Isaiah the prophet had predicted: "Lord, who will believe us? Who will accept God's mighty miracles as proof?" <sup>39</sup> But they couldn't believe, for as Isaiah also said: <sup>40</sup> "God has blinded their eyes and hardened their hearts so that they can neither see nor understand nor turn to me to heal them." <sup>41</sup> Isaiah was referring to Jesus when he made this prediction, for he had seen a vision of the Messiah's glory.

<sup>42</sup> However, even many of the Jewish leaders believed him to be the Messiah but wouldn't admit it to anyone because of their fear that the

Pharisees would excommunicate them from the synagogue; 43 for they loved the praise of men more than the praise of God.

44 Jesus shouted to the crowds, "If you trust me, you are really trusting God. 45 For when you see me, you are seeing the one who sent me. 46 I have come as a Light to shine in this dark world, so that all who put their trust in me will no longer wander in the darkness. 47 If anyone hears me and doesn't obey me, I am not his judge—for I have come to save the world and not to judge it. 48 But all who reject me and my message will be judged at the Day of Judgment by the truths I have spoken. 49 For these are not my own ideas, but I have told you what the Father said to tell you. 50 And I know his instructions lead to eternal life; so whatever he tells me to say, I say!"

**13** Jesus knew on the evening of Passover Day that it would be his last night on earth before returning to his Father. During supper the devil had already suggested to Judas Iscariot, Simon's son, that this was the night to carry out his plan to betray Jesus. Jesus knew that the Father had given him everything and that he had come from God and would return to God. And how he loved his disciples! 4 So he got up from the supper table, took off his robe, wrapped a towel around his loins, 5 poured water into a basin, and began to wash the disciples' feet and to wipe them with the towel he had around him.

6 When he came to Simon Peter, Peter said to

him, "Master, you shouldn't be washing our feet like this!"

7 Jesus replied, "You don't understand now why I am doing it; some day you will."

8 "No," Peter protested, "you shall never wash my feet!"

"But if I don't, you can't be my partner," Jesus replied.

9 Simon Peter exclaimed, "Then wash my hands and head as well—not just my feet!"

10 Jesus replied, "One who has bathed all over needs only to have his feet washed to be entirely clean. Now you are clean—but that isn't true of everyone here." 11 For Jesus knew who would betray him. That is what he meant when he said, "Not all of you are clean."

12 After washing their feet he put on his robe again and sat down and asked, "Do you understand what I was doing? 13 You call me 'Master' and 'Lord,' and you do well to say it, for it is true. 14 And since I, the Lord and Teacher, have washed your feet, you ought to wash each other's feet. 15 I have given you an example to follow: do as I have done to you. 16 How true it is that a servant is not greater than his master. Nor is the messenger more important than the one who sends him. 17 You know these things—now do them! That is the path of blessing.

18 "I am not saying these things to all of you; I know so well each one of you I chose. The Scripture declares, 'One who eats supper with me will betray me,' and this will soon come true. 19 I tell you this now so that when it happens, you will believe on me.

20 "Truly, anyone welcoming my messenger is

welcoming me. And to welcome me is to welcome the Father who sent me."

²¹ Now Jesus was in great anguish of spirit and exclaimed, "Yes, it is true—one of you will betray me." ²² The disciples looked at each other, wondering whom he could mean. ²³ Since I was sitting next to Jesus at the table, being his closest friend, ²⁴ Simon Peter motioned to me to ask him who it was who would do this terrible deed.

²⁵ So I turned and asked him, "Lord, who is it?"

²⁶ He told me, "It is the one I honor by giving the bread dipped in the sauce."

And when he had dipped it, he gave it to Judas, son of Simon Iscariot.

²⁷ As soon as Judas had eaten it, Satan entered into him. Then Jesus told him, "Hurry—do it now."

²⁸ None of the others at the table knew what Jesus meant. ²⁹ Some thought that since Judas was their treasurer, Jesus was telling him to go and pay for the food or to give some money to the poor. ³⁰ Judas left at once, going out into the night.

³¹ As soon as Judas left the room, Jesus said, "My time has come; the glory of God will soon surround me—and God shall receive great praise because of all that happens to me. ³² And God shall give me his own glory, and this so very soon. ³³ Dear, dear children, how brief are these moments before I must go away and leave you! Then, though you search for me, you cannot come to me—just as I told the Jewish leaders.

³⁴ "And so I am giving a new commandment to you now—love each other just as much as I love

you. ³⁵ Your strong love for each other will prove to the world that you are my disciples."

³⁶ Simon Peter said, "Master, where are you going?"

And Jesus replied, "You can't go with me now; but you will follow me later."

³⁷ "But why can't I come now?" he asked, "for I am ready to die for you."

³⁸ Jesus answered, "Die for me? No—three times before the cock crows tomorrow morning, you will deny that you even know me!

**14** "Let not your heart be troubled. You are trusting God, now trust in me. ²,³ There are many homes up there where my Father lives, and I am going to prepare them for your coming. When everything is ready, then I will come and get you, so that you can always be with me where I am. If this weren't so, I would tell you plainly. ⁴ And you know where I am going and how to get there."

⁵ "No, we don't," Thomas said. "We haven't any idea where you are going, so how can we know the way?"

⁶ Jesus told him, "I am the Way—yes, and the Truth and the Life. No one can get to the Father except by means of me. ⁷ If you had known who I am, then you would have known who my Father is. From now on you know him—and have seen him!"

⁸ Philip said, "Sir, show us the Father and we will be satisfied."

⁹ Jesus replied, "Don't you even yet know who

I am, Philip, even after all this time I have been with you? Anyone who has seen me has seen the Father! So why are you asking to see him? [10] Don't you believe that I am in the Father and the Father is in me? The words I say are not my own but are from my Father who lives in me. And he does his work through me. [11] Just believe it—that I am in the Father and the Father is in me. Or else believe it because of the mighty miracles you have seen me do.

[12, 13] "In solemn truth I tell you, anyone believing in me shall do the same miracles I have done, and even greater ones, because I am going to be with the Father. You can ask him for *anything*, using my name, and I will do it, for this will bring praise to the Father because of what I, the Son, will do for you. [14] Yes, ask *anything*, using my name, and I will do it!

[15, 16] "If you love me, obey me; and I will ask the Father and he will give you another Comforter, and he will never leave you. [17] He is the Holy Spirit, the Spirit who leads into all truth. The world at large cannot receive him, for it isn't looking for him and doesn't recognize him. But you do, for he lives with you now and some day shall be in you. [18] No, I will not abandon you or leave you as orphans in the storm—I will come to you. [19] In just a little while I will be gone from the world, but I will still be present with you. For I will live again—and you will too. [20] When I come back to life again, you will know that I am in my Father, and you in me, and I in you. [21] The one who obeys me is the one who loves me; and because he loves me, my Father

will love him; and I will too, and I will reveal myself to him."

²² Judas (not Judas Iscariot, but his other disciple with that name) said to him, "Sir, why are you going to reveal yourself only to us disciples and not to the world at large?"

²³ Jesus replied, "Because I will only reveal myself to those who love me and obey me. The Father will love them too, and we will come to them and live with them. ²⁴ Anyone who doesn't obey me doesn't love me. And remember, I am not making up this answer to your question! It is the answer given by the Father who sent me.

²⁵ "I am telling you these things now while I am still with you. ²⁶ But when the Father sends the Comforter instead of me—and by the Comforter I mean the Holy Spirit—he will teach you much, as well as remind you of everything I myself have told you.

²⁷ "I am leaving you with a gift—peace of mind and heart! And the peace I give isn't fragile like the peace the world gives. So don't be troubled or afraid. ²⁸ Remember what I told you—I am going away, but I will come back to you again. If you really love me, you will be very happy for me, for now I can go to the Father, who is greater than I am. ²⁹ I have told you these things before they happen so that when they do, you will believe [in me].

³⁰ "I don't have much more time to talk to you, for the evil prince of this world approaches. He has no power over me, ³¹ but I will freely do what the Father requires of me so that the world will know that I love the Father. Come, let's be going.

**15** "I am the true Vine, and my Father is the Gardener. [2] He lops off every branch that doesn't produce. And he prunes those branches that bear fruit for even larger crops. [3] He has already tended you by pruning you back for greater strength and usefulness by means of the commands I gave you. [4] Take care to live in me, and let me live in you. For a branch can't produce fruit when severed from the vine. Nor can you be fruitful apart from me.

[5] "Yes, I am the Vine; you are the branches. Whoever lives in me and I in him shall produce a large crop of fruit. For apart from me you can't do a thing. [6] If anyone separates from me, he is thrown away like a useless branch, withers, and is gathered into a pile with all the others and burned. [7] But if you stay in me and obey my commands, you may ask any request you like, and it will be granted! [8] My true disciples produce bountiful harvests. This brings great glory to my Father.

[9] "I have loved you even as the Father has loved me. Live within my love. [10] When you obey me you are living in my love, just as I obey my Father and live in his love. [11] I have told you this so that you will be filled with my joy. Yes, your cup of joy will overflow! [12] I demand that you love each other as much as I love you. [13] And here is how to measure it—the greatest love is shown when a person lays down his life for his friends; [14] and you are my friends if you obey me. [15] I no longer call you slaves, for a master doesn't confide in his slaves; now you are my

friends, proved by the fact that I have told you everything the Father told me.

16 "You didn't choose me! I chose you! I appointed you to go and produce lovely fruit always, so that no matter what you ask for from the Father, using my name, he will give it to you. 17 I demand that you love each other, 18 for you get enough hate from the world! But then, it hated me before it hated you. 19 The world would love you if you belonged to it; but you don't—for I chose you to come out of the world, and so it hates you. 20 Do you remember what I told you? 'A slave isn't greater than his master!' So since they persecuted me, naturally they will persecute you. And if they had listened to me, they would listen to you! 21 The people of the world will persecute you because you belong to me, for they don't know God who sent me.

22 "They would not be guilty if I had not come and spoken to them. But now they have no excuse for their sin. 23 Anyone hating me is also hating my Father. 24 If I hadn't done such mighty miracles among them they would not be counted guilty. But as it is, they saw these miracles and yet they hated both of us—me and my Father. 25 This has fulfilled what the prophets said concerning the Messiah, 'They hated me without reason.'

26 "But I will send you the Comforter—the Holy Spirit, the source of all truth. He will come to you from the Father and will tell you all about me. 27 And you also must tell everyone about me, because you have been with me from the beginning.

# 16

"I have told you these things so that you won't be staggered [by all that lies ahead]. [2] For you will be excommunicated from the synagogues, and indeed the time is coming when those who kill you will think they are doing God a service. [3] This is because they have never known the Father or me. [4] Yes, I'm telling you these things now so that when they happen you will remember I warned you. I didn't tell you earlier because I was going to be with you for a while longer.

[5] "But now I am going away to the one who sent me; and none of you seems interested in the purpose of my going; none wonders why. [6] Instead you are only filled with sorrow. [7] But the fact of the matter is that it is best for you that I go away, for if I don't, the Comforter won't come. If I do, he will—for I will send him to you.

[8] "And when he has come he will convince the world of its sin, and of the availability of God's goodness, and of deliverance from judgment. [9] The world's sin is unbelief in me; [10] there is righteousness available because I go to the Father and you shall see me no more; [11] there is deliverance from judgment because the prince of this world has already been judged.

[12] "Oh, there is so much more I want to tell you, but you can't understand it now. [13] When the Holy Spirit, who is truth, comes, he shall guide you into all truth, for he will not be presenting his own ideas, but will be passing on to you what he has heard. He will tell you about the future. [14] He shall praise me and bring me

great honor by showing you my glory. ¹⁵ All the Father's glory is mine; this is what I mean when I say that he will show you my glory.

¹⁶ "In just a little while I will be gone, and you will see me no more; but just a little while after that, and you will see me again!"

¹⁷,¹⁸ "Whatever is he saying?" some of his disciples asked. "What is this about 'going to the Father'? We don't know what he means."

¹⁹ Jesus realized they wanted to ask him so he said, "Are you asking yourselves what I mean? ²⁰ The world will greatly rejoice over what is going to happen to me, and you will weep. But your weeping shall suddenly be turned to wonderful joy [when you see me again]. ²¹ It will be the same joy as that of a woman in labor when her child is born—her anguish gives place to rapturous joy and the pain is forgotten. ²² You have sorrow now, but I will see you again and then you will rejoice; and no one can rob you of that joy. ²³ At that time you won't need to ask me for anything, for you can go directly to the Father and ask him, and he will give you what you ask for because you use my name. ²⁴ You haven't tried this before, [but begin now]. Ask, using my name, and you will receive, and your cup of joy will overflow.

²⁵ "I have spoken of these matters very guardedly, but the time will come when this will not be necessary and I will tell you plainly all about the Father. ²⁶ Then you will present your petitions over my signature! And I won't need to ask the Father to grant you these requests, ²⁷ for the Father himself loves you dearly because you love me and believe that I came from the Father.

²⁸ Yes, I came from the Father into the world and will leave the world and return to the Father."

²⁹ "At last you are speaking plainly," his disciples said, "and not in riddles. ³⁰ Now we understand that you know everything and don't need anyone to tell you anything. From this we believe that you came from God."

³¹ "Do you finally believe this?" Jesus asked. ³² "But the time is coming—in fact, it is here—when you will be scattered, each one returning to his own home, leaving me alone. Yet I will not be alone, for the Father is with me. ³³ I have told you all this so that you will have peace of heart and mind. Here on earth you will have many trials and sorrows; but cheer up, for I have overcome the world."

**17** When Jesus had finished saying all these things he looked up to heaven and said, "Father, the time has come. Reveal the glory of your Son so that he can give the glory back to you. ² For you have given him authority over every man and woman in all the earth. He gives eternal life to each one you have given him. ³ And this is the way to have eternal life—by knowing you, the only true God, and Jesus Christ, the one you sent to earth! ⁴ I brought glory to you here on earth by doing everything you told me to. ⁵ And now, Father, reveal my glory as I stand in your presence, the glory we shared before the world began.

⁶ "I have told these men all about you. They were in the world, but then you gave them to me. Actually, they were always yours, and you gave

them to me; and they have obeyed you. 7 Now
they know that everything I have is a gift from
you, 8 for I have passed on to them the
commands you gave me; and they accepted them
and know of a certainty that I came down to
earth from you, and they believe you sent me.

9 "My plea is not for the world but for those
you have given me because they belong to you.
10 And all of them, since they are mine, belong to
you; and you have given them back to me with
everything else of yours, and so *they are my
glory!* 11 Now I am leaving the world, and leaving
them behind, and coming to you. Holy Father,
keep them in your own care—all those you have
given me—so that they will be united just as we
are, with none missing. 12 During my time here I
have kept safe within your family all of these
you gave me. I guarded them so that not one
perished, except the son of hell, as the Scriptures
foretold.

13 "And now I am coming to you. I have told
them many things while I was with them so that
they would be filled with my joy. 14 I have given
them your commands. And the world hates them
because they don't fit in with it, just as I don't.
15 I'm not asking you to take them out of the
world, but to keep them safe from Satan's power.
16 They are not part of this world any more than
I am. 17 Make them pure and holy through
teaching them your words of truth. 18 As you
sent me into the world, I am sending them into
the world, 19 and I consecrate myself to meet
their need for growth in truth and holiness.

20 "I am not praying for these alone but also
for the future believers who will come to me

because of the testimony of these. [21] My prayer for all of them is that they will be of one heart and mind, just as you and I are, Father—that just as you are in me and I am in you, so they will be in us, and the world will believe you sent me.

[22] "I have given them the glory you gave me— the glorious unity of being one, as we are— [23] I in them and you in me, all being perfected into one—so that the world will know you sent me and will understand that you love them as much as you love me. [24] Father, I want them with me— these you've given me—so that they can see my glory. You gave me the glory because you loved me before the world began!

[25] "O righteous Father, the world doesn't know you, but I do; and these disciples know you sent me. [26] And I have revealed you to them, and will keep on revealing you so that the mighty love you have for me may be in them, and I in them."

**18** After saying these things Jesus crossed the Kidron ravine with his disciples and entered a grove of olive trees. [2] Judas, the betrayer, knew this place, for Jesus had gone there many times with his disciples.

[3] The chief priests and Pharisees had given Judas a squad of soldiers and police to accompany him. Now with blazing torches, lanterns, and weapons they arrived at the olive grove.

[4, 5] Jesus fully realized all that was going to

happen to him. Stepping forward to meet them he asked, "Whom are you looking for?"

"Jesus of Nazareth," they replied.

"I am he," Jesus said. 6 And as he said it, they all fell backwards to the ground!

7 Once more he asked them, "Whom are you searching for?"

And again they replied, "Jesus of Nazareth."

8 "I told you I am he," Jesus said; "and since I am the one you are after, let these others go." 9 He did this to carry out the prophecy he had just made, "I have not lost a single one of those you gave me. . . ."

10 Then Simon Peter drew a sword and slashed off the right ear of Malchus, the High Priest's servant.

11 But Jesus said to Peter, "Put your sword away. Shall I not drink from the cup the Father has given me?"

12 So the Jewish police, with the soldiers and their lieutenant, arrested Jesus and tied him. 13 First they took him to Annas, the father-in-law of Caiaphas, the High Priest that year. 14 Caiaphas was the one who told the other Jewish leaders, "Better that one should die for all."

15 Simon Peter followed along behind, as did another of the disciples who was acquainted with the High Priest. So that other disciple was permitted into the courtyard along with Jesus, 16 while Peter stood outside the gate. Then the other disciple spoke to the girl watching at the gate, and she let Peter in. 17 The girl asked Peter, "Aren't you one of Jesus' disciples?"

"No," he said, "I am not!"

¹⁸ The police and the household servants were standing around a fire they had made, for it was cold. And Peter stood there with them, warming himself.

¹⁹ Inside, the High Priest began asking Jesus about his followers and what he had been teaching them.

²⁰ Jesus replied, "What I teach is widely known, for I have preached regularly in the synagogue and Temple; I have been heard by all the Jewish leaders and teach nothing in private that I have not said in public. ²¹ Why are you asking me this question? Ask those who heard me. You have some of them here. They know what I said."

²² One of the soldiers standing there struck Jesus with his fist. "Is that the way to answer the High Priest?" he demanded.

²³ "If I lied, prove it," Jesus replied. "Should you hit a man for telling the truth?"

²⁴ Then Annas sent Jesus, bound, to Caiaphas the High Priest.

²⁵ Meanwhile, as Simon Peter was standing by the fire, he was asked again, "Aren't you one of his disciples?"

"Of course not," he replied.

²⁶ But one of the household slaves of the High Priest—a relative of the man whose ear Peter had cut off—asked, "Didn't I see you out there in the olive grove with Jesus?"

²⁷ Again Peter denied it. And immediately a rooster crowed.

²⁸ Jesus' trial before Caiaphas ended in the early hours of the morning. Next he was taken to

the palace of the Roman governor. His accusers wouldn't go in themselves for that would "defile" them, they said, and they wouldn't be allowed to eat the Passover lamb. <sup>29</sup> So Pilate, the governor, went out to them and asked, "What is your charge against this man? What are you accusing him of doing?"

<sup>30</sup> "We wouldn't have arrested him if he weren't a criminal!" they retorted.

<sup>31</sup> "Then take him away and judge him yourselves by your own laws," Pilate told them.

"But we want him crucified," they demanded, "and your approval is required." <sup>32</sup> This fulfilled Jesus' prediction concerning the method of his execution.

<sup>33</sup> Then Pilate went back into the palace and called for Jesus to be brought to him. "Are you the King of the Jews?" he asked him.

<sup>34</sup> " 'King' as *you* use the word or as the *Jews* use it?" Jesus asked.

<sup>35</sup> "Am I a Jew?" Pilate retorted. "Your own people and their chief priests brought you here. Why? What have you done?"

<sup>36</sup> Then Jesus answered, "I am not an earthly king. If I were, my followers would have fought when I was arrested by the Jewish leaders. But my Kingdom is not of the world."

<sup>37</sup> Pilate replied, "But you are a king then?"

"Yes," Jesus said. "I was born for that purpose. And I came to bring truth to the world. All who love the truth are my followers."

<sup>38</sup> "What is truth?" Pilate exclaimed. Then he went out again to the people and told them, "He is not guilty of any crime. <sup>39</sup> But you have a

custom of asking me to release someone from prison each year at Passover. So if you want me to, I'll release the 'King of the Jews.' "

40 But they screamed back. "No! Not this man, but Barabbas!" Barabbas was a robber.

**19** Then Pilate laid open Jesus' back with a leaded whip, 2 and the soldiers made a crown of thorns and placed it on his head and robed him in royal purple. 3 "Hail, 'King of the Jews!' " they mocked, and struck him with their fists.

4 Pilate went outside again and said to the Jews, "I am going to bring him out to you now, but understand clearly that I find him *not guilty.*"

5 Then Jesus came out wearing the crown of thorns and the purple robe. And Pilate said, "Behold the man!"

6 At sight of him the chief priests and Jewish officials began yelling, "Crucify! Crucify!"

"*You* crucify him," Pilate said. "I find him *not guilty.*"

7 They replied, "By our laws he ought to die because he called himself the Son of God."

8 When Pilate heard this, he was more frightened than ever. 9 He took Jesus back into the palace again and asked him, "Where are you from?" but Jesus gave no answer.

10 "You won't talk to me?" Pilate demanded. "Don't you realize that I have the power to release you or to crucify you?"

11 Then Jesus said, "You would have no power at all over me unless it were given to you from

above. So those who brought me to you have the greater sin."

¹² Then Pilate tried to release him, but the Jewish leaders told him, "If you release this man, you are no friend of Caesar's. Anyone who declares himself a king is a rebel against Caesar."

¹³ At these words Pilate brought Jesus out to them again and sat down at the judgment bench on the stone-paved platform. ¹⁴ It was now about noon of the day before Passover.

And Pilate said to the Jews, "Here is your king!"

¹⁵ "Away with him," they yelled. "Away with him—crucify him!"

"What? Crucify your king?" Pilate asked.

"We have no king but Caesar," the chief priests shouted back.

¹⁶ Then Pilate gave Jesus to them to be crucified.

¹⁷ So they had him at last, and he was taken out of the city, carrying his cross to the place known as "The Skull," in Hebrew, "Golgotha." ¹⁸ There they crucified him and two others with him, one on either side, with Jesus between them. ¹⁹ And Pilate posted a sign over him reading, "Jesus of Nazareth, the King of the Jews." ²⁰ The place where Jesus was crucified was near the city; and the signboard was written in Hebrew, Latin, and Greek, so that many people read it.

²¹ Then the chief priests said to Pilate, "Change it from 'The King of the Jews' to '*He said,* I am King of the Jews.' "

²² Pilate replied, "What I have written, I have written. It stays exactly as it is."

²³, ²⁴ When the soldiers had crucified Jesus, they

put his garments into four piles, one for each of
them. But they said, "Let's not tear up his robe,"
for it was seamless. "Let's throw dice to see who
gets it." This fulfilled the Scripture that says,

"They divided my clothes among them, and
cast lots for my robe." ²⁵ So that is what they
did.

Standing near the cross were Jesus' mother,
Mary, his aunt, the wife of Cleopas, and Mary
Magdalene. ²⁶ When Jesus saw his mother
standing there beside me, his close friend, he said
to her, "He is your son."

²⁷ And to me he said, "She is your mother!"
And from then on I took her into my home.

²⁸ Jesus knew that everything was now
finished, and to fulfill the Scriptures said, "I'm
thirsty." ²⁹ A jar of sour wine was sitting there,
so a sponge was soaked in it and put on a hyssop
branch and held up to his lips.

³⁰ When Jesus had tasted it, he said, "It is
finished," and bowed his head and dismissed his
spirit.

³¹ The Jewish leaders didn't want the victims
hanging there the next day, which was the
Sabbath (and a very special Sabbath at that, for
it was the Passover), so they asked Pilate to
order the legs of the men broken to hasten death;
then their bodies could be taken down. ³² So the
soldiers came and broke the legs of the two men
crucified with Jesus; ³³ but when they came to
him, they saw that he was dead already, so they
didn't break his. ³⁴ However, one of the soldiers
pierced his side with a spear, and blood and
water flowed out. ³⁵ I saw all this myself and
have given an accurate report so that you also

can believe. [36, 37] The soldiers did this in
fulfillment of the Scripture that says, "Not one of
his bones shall be broken," and, "They shall look
on him whom they pierced."

[38] Afterwards Joseph of Arimathea, who had
been a secret disciple of Jesus for fear of the
Jewish leaders, boldly asked Pilate for
permission to take Jesus' body down; and Pilate
told him to go ahead. So he came and took it
away. [39] Nicodemus, the man who had come to
Jesus at night, came too, bringing a hundred
pounds of embalming ointment made from myrrh
and aloes. [40] Together they wrapped Jesus' body
in a long linen cloth saturated with the spices, as
is the Jewish custom of burial. [41] The place of
crucifixion was near a grove of trees, where there
was a new tomb, never used before. [42] And so,
because of the need for haste before the Sabbath,
and because the tomb was close at hand, they
laid him there.

**20** Early Sunday morning, while it was
still dark, Mary Magdalene came to
the tomb and found that the stone
was rolled aside from the entrance.

[2] She ran and found Simon Peter and me and
said, "They have taken the Lord's body out of
the tomb, and I don't know where they have put
him!"

[3, 4] We ran to the tomb to see; I outran Peter
and got there first, [5] and stooped and looked in
and saw the linen cloth lying there, but I didn't
go in. [6] Then Simon Peter arrived and went on
inside. He also noticed the cloth lying there,

[7] while the swath that had covered Jesus' head was rolled up in a bundle and was lying at the side. [8] Then I went in too, and saw, and believed [that he had risen]—[9] for until then we hadn't realized that the Scriptures said he would come to life again!

[10] We went on home, [11] and by that time Mary had returned to the tomb and was standing outside crying. And as she wept, she stooped and looked in [12] and saw two white-robed angels sitting at the head and foot of the place where the body of Jesus had been lying.

[13] "Why are you crying?" the angels asked her.

"Because they have taken away my Lord," she replied, "and I don't know where they have put him."

[14] She glanced over her shoulder and saw someone standing behind her. It was Jesus, but she didn't recognize him!

[15] "Why are you crying?" he asked her. "Whom are you looking for?"

She thought he was the gardener. "Sir," she said, "if you have taken him away, tell me where you have put him, and I will go and get him."

[16] "Mary!" Jesus said. She turned toward him.

"Master!" she exclaimed.

[17] "Don't touch me," he cautioned, "for I haven't yet ascended to the Father. But go find my brothers and tell them that I ascend to my Father and your Father, my God and your God."

[18] Mary Magdalene found the disciples and told them, "I have seen the Lord!" Then she gave them his message.

[19] That evening the disciples were meeting

behind locked doors, in fear of the Jewish leaders, when suddenly Jesus was standing there among them! After greeting them, [20] he showed them his hands and side. And how wonderful was their joy as they saw their Lord!

[21] He spoke to them again and said, "As the Father has sent me, even so I am sending you." [22] Then he breathed on them and told them, "Receive the Holy Spirit. [23] If you forgive anyone's sins, they are forgiven. If you refuse to forgive them, they are unforgiven."

[24] One of the disciples, Thomas, "The Twin," was not there at the time with the others. [25] When they kept telling him, "We have seen the Lord," he replied, "I won't believe it unless I see the nail wounds in his hands—and put my fingers into them—and place my hand into his side."

[26] Eight days later the disciples were together again, and this time Thomas was with them. The doors were locked; but suddenly, as before, Jesus was standing among them and greeting them.

[27] Then he said to Thomas, "Put your finger into my hands. Put your hand into my side. Don't be faithless any longer. Believe!"

[28] "My Lord and my God!" Thomas said.

[29] Then Jesus told him, "You believe because you have seen me. But blessed are those who haven't seen me and believe anyway."

[30, 31] Jesus' disciples saw him do many other miracles besides the ones told about in this book, but these are recorded so that you will believe that he is the Messiah, the Son of God, and that believing in him you will have life.

# 21

Later Jesus appeared again to the disciples beside the Lake of Galilee. This is how it happened:

2 A group of us were there—Simon Peter, Thomas, "The Twin," Nathanael from Cana in Galilee, my brother James and I and two other disciples.

3 Simon Peter said, "I'm going fishing."

"We'll come too," we all said. We did, but caught nothing all night. 4 At dawn we saw a man standing on the beach but couldn't see who he was.

5 He called, "Any fish, boys?"

"No," we replied.

6 Then he said, "Throw out your net on the right-hand side of the boat, and you'll get plenty of them!" So we did, and couldn't draw in the net because of the weight of the fish, there were so many!

7 Then I said to Peter, "It is the Lord!" At that, Simon Peter put on his tunic (for he was stripped to the waist) and jumped into the water [and swam ashore]. 8 The rest of us stayed in the boat and pulled the loaded net to the beach, about 300 feet away. 9 When we got there, we saw that a fire was kindled and fish were frying over it, and there was bread.

10 "Bring some of the fish you've just caught," Jesus said. 11 So Simon Peter went out and dragged the net ashore. By his count there were 153 large fish; and yet the net hadn't torn.

12 "Now come and have some breakfast!" Jesus said; and none of us dared ask him if he really was the Lord, for we were quite sure of it.

¹³ Then Jesus went around serving us the bread and fish.

¹⁴ This was the third time Jesus had appeared to us since his return from the dead.

¹⁵ After breakfast Jesus said to Simon Peter, "Simon, son of John, do you love me more than these others?"

"Yes," Peter replied, "You know I am your friend."

"Then feed my lambs," Jesus told him.

¹⁶ Jesus repeated the question: "Simon, son of John, do you *really* love me?"

"Yes, Lord," Peter said, "you know I am your friend."

"Then take care of my sheep," Jesus said.

¹⁷ Once more he asked him, "Simon, son of John, are you even my friend?"

Peter was grieved at the way Jesus asked the question this third time. "Lord, you know my heart; you know I am," he said.

Jesus said, "Then feed my little sheep. ¹⁸ When you were young, you were able to do as you liked and go wherever you wanted to; but when you are old, you will stretch out your hands and others will direct you and take you where you don't want to go." ¹⁹ Jesus said this to let him know what kind of death he would die to glorify God. Then Jesus told him, "Follow me."

²⁰ Peter turned around and saw the disciple Jesus loved following, the one who had leaned around at supper that time to ask Jesus, "Master, which of us will betray you?" ²¹ Peter asked Jesus, "What about him, Lord? What sort of death will he die?"

<sup>22</sup> Jesus replied, "If I want him to live until I return, what is that to you? *You* follow me."

<sup>23</sup> So the rumor spread among the brotherhood that that disciple wouldn't die! But that isn't what Jesus said at all! He only said, "If I want him to live until I come, what is that to you?"

<sup>24</sup> *I am that disciple!* I saw these events and have recorded them here. And we all know that my account of these things is accurate.

<sup>25</sup> And I suppose that if all the other events in Jesus' life were written, the whole world could hardly contain the books!

## Other Resources

AUDIO CASSETTE TAPES
Related teachings by Jack Hayford are available through the SoundWord Tape Ministry. The following is a suggested list that correlates closely with the theme of water baptism.

| TITLE | TAPE NUMBER |
|-------|-------------|
| "Water Baptism" | 49 |
| "Believe and Be Baptized" | 2086 |
| "Baptized into Life-giving Possibilities" | 2090 |
| "Saint, Be Baptized" | 988 |
| "Saint, Live Baptized" | 990 |

Please refer to the tape number when ordering. These audio cassette tapes, as well as a complete catalog of tapes by Jack Hayford, can be obtained by writing to: SoundWord Tape Ministry, 14300 Sherman Way, Van Nuys, CA 91405-2499.

VIDEOTAPES
Videotapes for use in homes, Bible studies, small group meetings, and churches may be special ordered. For information and a catalog of current listings, please write to: Living Way Ministries, 14300 Sherman Way, Van Nuys, CA 91405-2499.

## Other Books by Jack Hayford

Along with *Newborn* there are several other booklets in this series by Jack Hayford available from Tyndale House Publishers.

*Daybreak*
A handbook on daily prayer that directs the reader to present all of his life and self to God. Jack Hayford discusses how believers can establish daily time with God, and he gives guidelines for preparing one's heart and day so that it becomes a daily habit to have a daybreak meeting with God.

*Prayerpath*
A new call has gone out around the world—a call to believers to unite in concerts of prayer, joining in faith for spiritual breakthrough on a global dimension. In *Prayerpath,* Jack Hayford takes readers step by step along the pathway of prayer, showing what Jesus taught about how to pray and how to live and grow in vital faith.

*Spirit-Filled*
Practical instruction on the person and power of the Spirit, teaching how, when, and where to put the spiritual gifts and graces to use in your life. Encourages the reader to open to the fullness of the Spirit of Christ and shows how to maintain wisdom and balance in daily Spirit-filled living.

The following book by Jack Hayford is also available from Tyndale House Publishers:

*The Visitor*
A study of the suffering of Christ that gives the reader an uncluttered insight into the reasons for and results of Christ's visit to mankind. A perceptive, on-target treatment that enables readers to meet the Visitor face to face, recognizing his endless love and accepting his purpose and plan in their lives.